Shauna Berglund-Immel

Susan Cobb

LeNae Gerig

Amy Gustafson

About the Designers:

Shauna Berglund-Immel works for Hot Off The Press as a Scrapbook Specialist and in-house designer. Shauna and her husband Dave live in Oregon with their children Spencer and Kaelin. Shauna collects children's books and loves sports of all kinds.

Susan Cobb is a talented Hot Off The Press designer, Scrapbook Specialist and technical editor who particularly enjoys drawing, painting and creating with paper. She lives in Oregon with her husband Brian, their two daughters and their cat.

LeNae Gerig lives in Oregon with her husband Chris, their daughter Lauren and their dog Bailey. LeNae is an in-house designer, Scrapbook Specialist and technical editor for Hot Off The Press. She likes to explore new crafts and search for antiques.

Amy Gustafson, the newest member of Hot Off The Press' design team, is a Scrapbook Specialist, calligrapher and paper crafter. Amy grew up in Oregon but now lives in France, where she is a teacher and missionary.

Production Credits:

✦ **President:** Paulette Jarvey
✦ **Vice President:** Teresa Nelson
✦ **Project editor:** Diane Weiner
✦ **Technical editor:** LeNae Gerig
✦ **Photographer:** John McNally
✦ **Graphic designers:** Jacie Pete, Carmalee Justis
✦ **Editor:** Lynda Hill
✦ **Digital imagers:** Larry Seith, Victoria Weber

The publisher and designers would like to thank the following companies for providing materials used in this publication:
✦ **Craf-T Products** for decorating chalks
✦ **Dixon Ticonderoga Co.** for Prang colored pencils
✦ **EK Success, Ltd.** for Zig Writer pens
✦ **Family Treasures** for craft punches
✦ **McGill, Inc.** for craft punches
✦ **Pentel of America** for Milky Gel Roller pens

published by:

HOT OFF THE PRESS INC.

For a color catalog of nearly 750 products, send $2.00 to:

HOT OFF THE PRESS INC.
1250 N.W. Third, Dept. B
Canby, Oregon 97013
phone (503) 266-9102
fax (503) 266-8749
http://www.paperpizazz.com

201 PAPER PIECING Patterns

FULL-SIZE PATTERNS READY FOR YOU!

IT'S A GIRL

PERFECT FOR:
- memory albums
- scrapbooks
- card making
- bulletin boards
- paper crafting

Table Of Contents

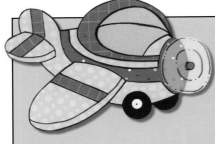

Paper piecing—the art of cutting and gluing papers into shapes—is a fun way to embellish your scrapbook pages, cards and other paper crafts. We at Hot Off The Press know how much you love paper piecing, so we created 201 patterns just for you! Simply collect the basic supplies, follow our step-by-step instructions (below) and you're on your way! Often paper piecing is done with solid colored papers, but of course we wanted more pizazz so most of these designs are shown with Paper Pizazz™ patterned papers. Just another option for you to consider! Where there's room, we've shown some sample album pages. Happy Scrapping!

Basic Supplies

- Paper Pizazz™ solid and patterned papers
- transfer paper
- straight-edged scissors
- tracing paper
- pencil
- ruler
- optional: decorating scissors, assorted craft punches, foam mounting tape, decorating chalk, cotton swab or sponge eye shadow applicator, stylus, X-acto® knife, cutting surface

How to Use Paper Piecing Patterns

1 Choose your pattern: This book has a pattern for almost any occasion! Remember, your finished piece will be the size of the pattern and not the size of the colored image.

2 Decide on your papers: The photo of the paper pieced design offers suggested papers and lists the Paper Pizazz™ books in which you can find those papers. Of course, you might want to change the papers to coordinate with your photographs. For example, you can cut the school girl's jumper (shown here) from a paper that resembles your little girl's favorite dress.

3 Trace the pattern: Lay a piece of tracing paper over the pattern in this book and use a pencil to go over all the black outlines and blue cutting lines (more about these in step 7). If you plan to trace the penwork details onto the design rather than draw them freehand, trace the gray penwork lines, too.

4 Transfer the pattern to patterned paper using one of two methods:
- Place the tracing on your patterned paper. Slip transfer paper beneath it and go over the lines with a pencil or stylus.
- Or, to avoid stray pencil marks on the paper, turn the tracing paper over (this is important—the design will be reversed) and place it on the back of your patterned paper. Slip transfer paper beneath it and go over the lines with a pencil or stylus.

5 Cut out the pattern pieces: On a few of the patterns in this book, such as Bear With Heart or Star (shown at left); our Scrapbook Specialists used pattern-edged scissors to cut out certain pattern pieces. You may do the same or cut a straight edge. In some cases, craft punches were used for small pattern pieces (such as the bear's nose). We've listed the punches used, but we also give patterns for the shapes so you don't have to purchase a punch.

6 Here's one option to help the pattern pieces stand out: Mat some or all of the pieces on solid colored paper. (For an example, see the Umbrella at right). Glue each piece to solid paper and trim around it, leaving a very narrow 1/16"-1/8" border. We'll use a ♥ to tell you when we've done this.

7. Assemble the pieces: Referring to the photo of the pieced item, arrange the pieces to make sure everything fits. If your pattern contains a blue line, such as on the Country Valentine boy's shirt (shown at right); cut along the line with an X-acto® knife or scissors and insert the indicated pattern piece or pieces into the cut.

insert overalls, stick and hand

8. Glue the pieces: When you're pleased with the design, glue the pieces into place. There are two options here: You might choose to glue the pieces directly onto your scrapbook page. Or, if you want to mat the finished design, glue the pieces to solid colored paper and trim around the design, leaving a 1/16"-1/8" border. When we use this matting technique on a design in this book, we'll tell you with a ★ followed by the mat color.

9. Add penwork such as faces, buttons, seams, etc. As an option, you may want to outline each piece just inside the cut edge to help it stand out in the final design. (We used this technique for the Teapot at left.) Use a fine-tip permanent black pen for most penwork, but for some pieces, we used colored gel pens or colored pencils (we'll tell you when and where). Use the photo of the paper-pieced item as a guide.

Tips

• Decorating chalks can add a delicate blush to cheeks such as the Scarecrow's. Place a small amount of pink chalk in the center of the cheek and use a cotton swab or sponge eye shadow applicator to gently blend the edges. Repeat if desired to darken the blush.

• You can quickly reduce or enlarge a pattern using a photocopier.

• For patterns with stripes such as those on the wings and tail fins of Airplane #1 (shown at right); cut each stripe a bit longer than the pattern calls for. Glue the stripes onto the project, then trim the ends even. This ensures that your stripes are exactly the right length.

• Don't be shy about customizing a design to fit your needs! For example, maybe your family hangs five stockings on the mantel each holiday season. Go ahead and use our Christmas fireplace pattern (page 65); but cut a wider fireplace, and add stockings. Or turn the Happy Birthday present (page 100) into a Christmas present simply by changing the papers.

• Using subtly textured or patterned papers instead of solids, as our Scrapbook Specialists did frequently in this book, will add an extra element of interest to your paper piecing. For example, the Top Hat (shown below) is pieced with black velvet patterned Paper Pizazz™. Isn't it smashing?

• For a fun, dimensional touch, use foam mounting tape to attach certain pattern pieces, such as noses, bows or flower centers.

• When working with vellum, handle it gently because creases will show up as permanent white lines. Most adhesives will show through, so use glue sparingly, apply it to the background paper rather than the vellum, and hide it behind another pattern piece if possible. Let liquid adhesive dry slightly before placing vellum onto it. A glue stick or glue pen works best.

 Look for more bright ideas—time saving tips, clever variations or scrapbook page suggestions—wherever you see this light bulb.

Acorn

- patterned *Paper Pizazz*™: brown plaid (*Great Outdoors*); burgundy with tri-dots*, green pin-stripe* (*Dots, Checks, Plaids & Stripes*)
- solid *Paper Pizazz*™: tan (*Plain Pastels*)
- black pen: Zig

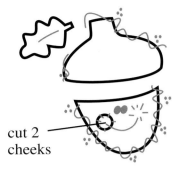

pattern by Lisa Williams

cut 2 cheeks

Airplane #1

- patterned *Paper Pizazz*™: red with hollow dots (*Bold & Bright*)*
- solid *Paper Pizazz*™: vellum (*Vellum Papers*); yellow (*Plain Pastels*); black (*Solid Jewel Tones*)
- black pen: Zig

★ Mat the finished piece on black.

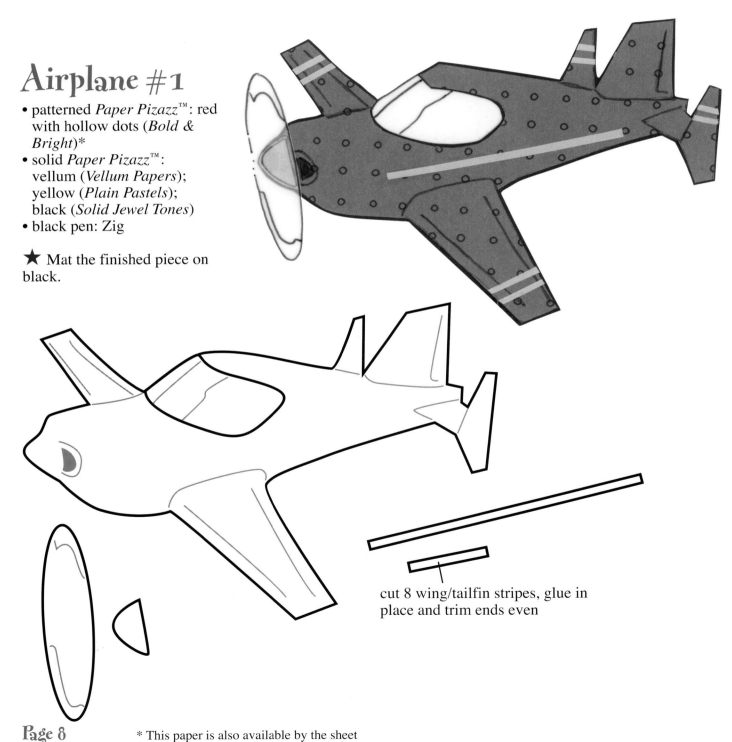

cut 8 wing/tailfin stripes, glue in place and trim ends even

* This paper is also available by the sheet

Airplane #2

- patterned *Paper Pizazz*™: yellow dots, blue checks (*Bright Tints*); colorful dots* (*Bright Great Backgrounds*)
- solid *Paper Pizazz*™: vellum (*Vellum Papers*); black (*Solid Jewel Tones*); white, light blue (*Plain Pastels*)
- black pen: Zig

♥ Mat each piece on black.

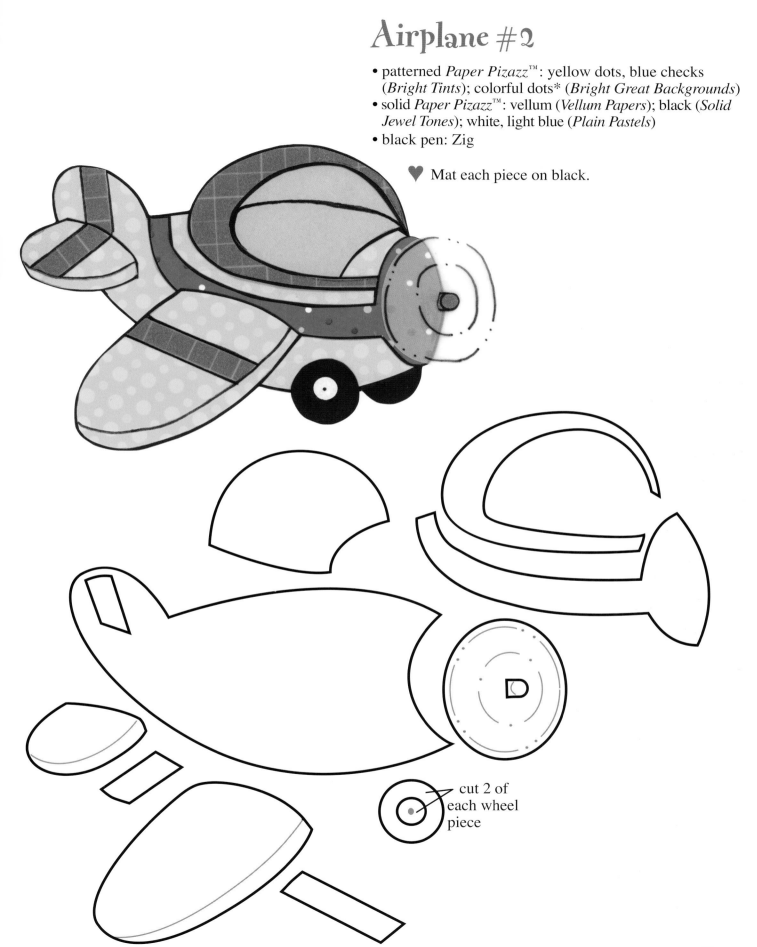

D

cut 2 of each wheel piece

Anchor

- patterned *Paper Pizazz*™: black and white swirl* (*Black & White Photos*);
  barnwood* (*Country*); gold sponged stars* (*Spattered, Crackled, Sponged*)
- solid *Paper Pizazz*™: black (*Solid Jewel Tones*)
- black pen: Zig

♥ Mat each piece on black.

For a shiny look, use specialty silver paper from *Paper Pizazz*™ *Heavy Metals Papers.*

* This paper is also available by the sheet

Angel with Star

- patterned *Paper Pizazz*™: green and white stripe, yellow with dots, blue with stars (*Lisa Williams' Blue, Yellow and Green*); pink and yellow plaid* (*Pastel Plaids*); ivory crackle (*Textured Papers*)
- solid *Paper Pizazz*™: specialty gold* (*Metallic Papers*); black (*Solid Jewel Tones*); pink, tan, yellow (*Plain Pastels*)
- ¼" hole punch: McGill, Inc.
- ½" circle punch: Marvy Uchida
- black pen: Zig

♥ Mat each piece on black.

pattern by Ruth Ninneman

cut 2 cheeks

Baby Buggy & Teddy Bear

- patterned *Paper Pizazz*™: red with white dots* (*Ho, Ho, Ho!!!*); yellow checks (*Bright Tints*); tan sponged with stars* (*Spattered, Crackled, Sponged*)
- solid *Paper Pizazz*™: black (*Solid Jewel Tones*); red, yellow (*Plain Brights*); white (*Plain Pastels*)
- ⅜" heart punch: Family Treasures
- black pen: Zig

♥ Mat each piece on black.

pattern by Teresa Nelson

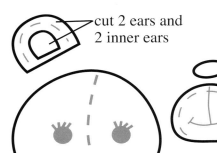

cut 2 ears and 2 inner ears

cut 8 wheel spokes

cut 2

cut 2

cut 9

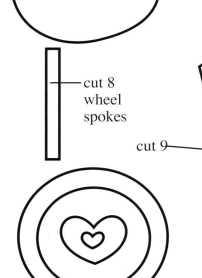

cut 2 of each wheel piece

* This paper is also available by the sheet

cut backpack in red

Backpack

- patterned *Paper Pizazz*™: school tartan* (*School Days*)
- solid *Paper Pizazz*™: red, yellow (*Plain Brights*)
- black pen: Zig

Ball, Baby

- patterned *Paper Pizazz*™: green swirl, pink and lavender diamonds (*Soft Tints*)
- black pen: Zig

* This paper is also available by the sheet

Ball, Beach

- patterned *Paper Pizazz*™: yellow dots (*Bright Tints*); teal suede, purple swirl, smudged blue, red with dots* (*Bright Great Backgrounds*)
- solid *Paper Pizazz*™: black (*Solid Jewel Tones*)
- black pen: Zig

★ Mat the finished piece on black.

💡 Use the beach ball with the sand bucket (page 106) for a fun beach page.

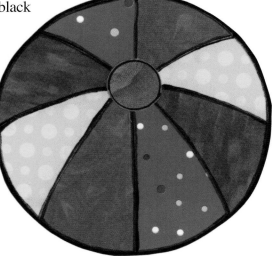

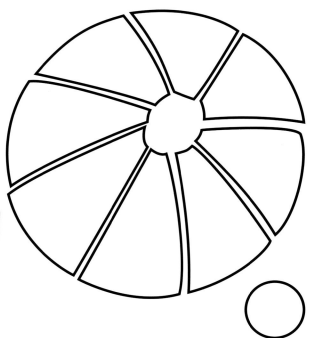

Ballerina

- patterned *Paper Pizazz*™: pink and yellow plaid* (*Pastel Plaids*)
- solid *Paper Pizazz*™: tan, pink, yellow, mint (*Plain Pastels*)
- ¼" hole punch: McGill, Inc.
- black pen: Zig

cut 2

cut 2

cut 7 roses

cut 11 leaves

cut 4

cut 2

pattern by Ruth Ninneman

* This paper is also available by the sheet

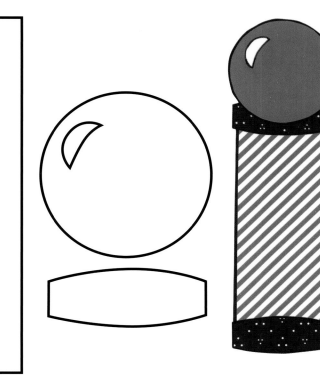

Barbershop Pole

- patterned *Paper Pizazz*™: red and white stripes* (*Ho, Ho, Ho!!!*); blue with tri-dots (*Dots, Checks, Plaids & Stripes*)
- solid *Paper Pizazz*™: red (*Plain Brights*); white (*Plain Pastels*); black (*Solid Jewel Tones*)

♥ Mat each piece on black.

Use with scissors (page 117) for a "My First Haircut" page.

Baseball Cap

- patterned *Paper Pizazz*™: red with stars,* red pinstripe,* red with tri-dots* (*Dots, Checks, Plaids & Stripes*)
- solid *Paper Pizazz*™: black (*Solid Jewel Tones*)
- black pen: Zig

★ Mat the finished piece on black.

Change the colors to match your favorite team's uniform.

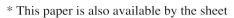

Basketball

- patterned *Paper Pizazz*™: basketballs* (*Sports*)
- solid *Paper Pizazz*™: black (*Solid Jewel Tones*)

★ Mat the finished piece on black.

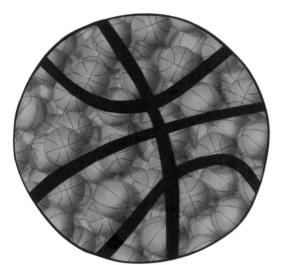

Bear Sitting with Balloons

- patterned *Paper Pizazz*™: burlap* (*Country*); burgundy with tri-dots*, burgundy stripe (*Dots, Checks, Plaids & Stripes*); forest green suede* (*Heritage Papers*)
- solid *Paper Pizazz*™: peach (*Solid Muted Colors*); black (*Solid Jewel Tones*)
- pink decorating chalk: Craf-T Products
- cotton swab
- black pen: Zig

pattern by Temple Garman

* This paper is also available by the sheet

Bear Hugging Balloon

- patterned *Paper Pizazz*™: burlap* (*Country*); green plaid* (*Dots, Checks, Plaids & Stripes*)
- solid *Paper Pizazz*™: peach (*Solid Muted Colors*); black (*Solid Jewel Tones*)
- pink decorating chalk: Craf-T Products
- cotton swab
- black pen: Zig

Pattern by Temple Garman

Bear with Pastel Balloons

- patterned *Paper Pizazz*™: pink and yellow plaid* (*Pastel Plaids*); yellow with dots (*Lisa Williams Blue, Yellow & Green*); light blue with tri-dots* (*Baby's First Year*)
- solid *Paper Pizazz*™: white, yellow (*Plain Pastels*)
- black pen: Zig

♥ Mat each piece on white.

cut 3 balloons

pattern by Ruth Ninneman

Bear with Star or Heart

- patterned *Paper Pizazz*™: brown crushed suede* (*Black & White Photos*); pink and yellow plaid* (*Pastel Plaids*); yellow with lavender dots* (*Dots, Checks, Plaids & Stripes*)
- solid *Paper Pizazz*™: white, dark pink (*Solid Pastels*)
- pink decorating chalk: Craf-T Products
- cotton swab
- ¼" hole punch: McGill, Inc.
- ripple scissors: Fiskars
- black pen: Zig

BE MINE

BOY

Personalize the heart or star with any message you like!

IT'S A GIRL

cut 2 paws

pattern by Nance Wihie-Kueneman

* This paper is also available by the sheet

cut 8

cut 2 for drum top and base

cut 4 for drum trim

cut 2 drumsticks

cut 2 sleeves

cut 2 stripes

cut 2 hat tails

Fourth of July Bear

- patterned *Paper Pizazz*™: navy tiles*, red stars* (*Dots, Checks, Plaids & Stripes*); red and white stripe* (*Ho, Ho, Ho!!!*); crocodile skin (*Textured Papers*); brown sponged (*Bj's Handpainted Papers*)
- solid *Paper Pizazz*™: white, light blue, tan (*Plain Pastels*); black (*Solid Jewel Tones*); specialty gold* (*Metallic Papers*)
- ¼" hole punch: McGill, Inc.
- black pen: Zig

pattern by Ruth Ninneman

♥ Mat each piece on black.

* This paper is also available by the sheet

Boy & Girl Bears

patterns by Ruth Ninneman

- patterned *Paper Pizazz*™: tan sponged (*Spattered, Crackled, Sponged*); pink dots, pink hearts and flowers (*Lisa Williams Pink, Lavender & Beige*); blue with stars (*Lisa Williams Blue, Yellow & Green*); yellow check (*Bright Tints*)
- solid *Paper Pizazz*™: white (*Plain Pastels*)
- ¼" hole punch: McGill, Inc.
- pink decorating chalk: Craf-T Products
- cotton swab
- black pen: Zig

cut 2 hands

cut 3 buttons

Bee

- patterned *Paper Pizazz*™: yellow dots (*Bright Tints*)
- solid *Paper Pizazz*™: black (*Solid Jewel Tones*); vellum (*Vellum Papers*)
- black pen: Zig

Add several bees to any of the Paper Pizazz™ floral sheets: roses, hydrangeas, daisies, etc.

cut 4 wings

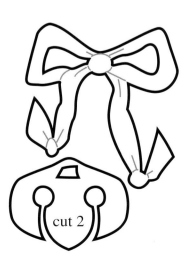

Jingle Bells

- patterned *Paper Pizazz*™: burgundy velvet (*"Velvet" Backgrounds*); ivory crackle (*Spattered, Crackled, Sponged*)
- solid *Paper Pizazz*™: black (*Solid Jewel Tones*)
- black pen: Zig

♥ Mat each piece on black.

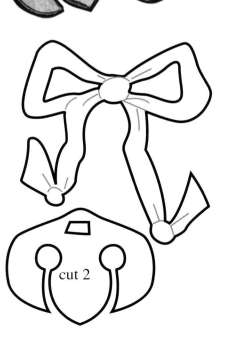

cut 2

cut 2

Of course the bells would also be perfect cut from our specialty silver or gold (available in *Heavy Metals Papers*) Paper Pizazz™. Both are also available by the sheet.

Wedding Bells

- patterned *Paper Pizazz*™: laser lace* (*Romantic Papers*); white moiré* (*Wedding*); pink satin* (*Pretty Papers*)
- solid *Paper Pizazz*™: ivory (*Plain Pastels*)

♥ Mat each piece on white.

Glue the laser lace to the moiré, then trace and cut out 2 bells.

cut 2

cut 2

cut 2

Notice how the pink satin Paper Pizazz™ gives dimension to the ribbon. It's also available in purple and white!

Bible

- patterned *Paper Pizazz*™: white moiré* (*Wedding*); burgundy with tri-dots* (*Dots, Checks, Plaids & Stripes*)
- solid *Paper Pizazz*™: specialty gold* (*Metallic Papers*)
- black glitter pen: Sakura

insert bookmark

* This paper is also available by the sheet

cut 2 of
all pieces

Cowboy Boots

- patterned *Paper Pizazz*™: alligator skin (*Wild Things*); leather (*Textured Papers*)
- solid *Paper Pizazz*™: black (*Solid Jewel Tones*)
- black pen: Zig
- white pen: Pentel

★ Mat the finished piece on black.

💡 Use the boots with the cowboy hat (page 78) for a Western-themed page.

Hiking Boot

- patterned *Paper Pizazz*™: leather (*Textured Papers*); brown plaid* (*The Great Outdoors*); burgundy velvet, green velvet (*"Velvet" Backgrounds*)
- solid *Paper Pizazz*™: tan (*Plain Pastels*); black (*Jewel Tones*)
- ⅜" hole punch: McGill, Inc.
- black pen: Zig

cut 5

* This paper is also available by the sheet

Baby Bottle

- patterned *Paper Pizazz*™: white moiré* (*Wedding*); blue stripe, yellow dot, pink check (*Soft Tints*)
- solid *Paper Pizazz*™: medium blue (*Plain Pastels*)
- black pen: Zig

 Write baby's birth date, weight and length on the bottle.

School Boy

- patterned *Paper Pizazz*™: denim*, (*Country*); colorful stripes* (*Birthday*)
- solid *Paper Pizazz*™: red, yellow (*Plain Brights*); tan, white, pink (*Plain Pastels*); black (*Solid Jewel Tones*)
- black pen: Zig

Cut out the body and dress him to make your own paper dolls!

cut 2 cheeks

cut 2 arms

pattern by Ruth Nimeman

* This paper is also available by the sheet

Bubbles

- patterned *Paper Pizazz*™: light blue with tri-dots* (*Baby's First Year*); colorful bubbles (*Bright Great Backgrounds*)
- solid *Paper Pizazz*™: yellow, white (*Plain Pastels*); black (*Solid Jewel Tones*)
- ¼" hole punch: McGill, Inc.
- black pen: Zig

Bugs

- patterned *Paper Pizazz*™: purple swirl, blue smudge (*Bright Great Backgrounds*)
- solid *Paper Pizazz*™: white, pink (*Plain Pastels*); vellum (*Vellum Papers*)
- purple decorating chalk: Craf-T Products
- cotton swab
- black pen: Zig

patterns by Annie Lang

* This paper is also available by the sheet

Plaid Bunny

- patterned *Paper Pizazz*™: green, yellow and pink plaid* (*Pastel Plaids*)
- solid *Paper Pizazz*™: white (*Plain Pastels*); sage green, mauve (*Solid Muted Colors*)
- black pen: Zig

♥ Mat the head, body, arms and legs on white.

💡 Here are six more Paper Pizazz™ plaids, all available by the sheet, that would look great on this bunny:

pattern by Teresa Nelson

* This paper is also available by the sheet

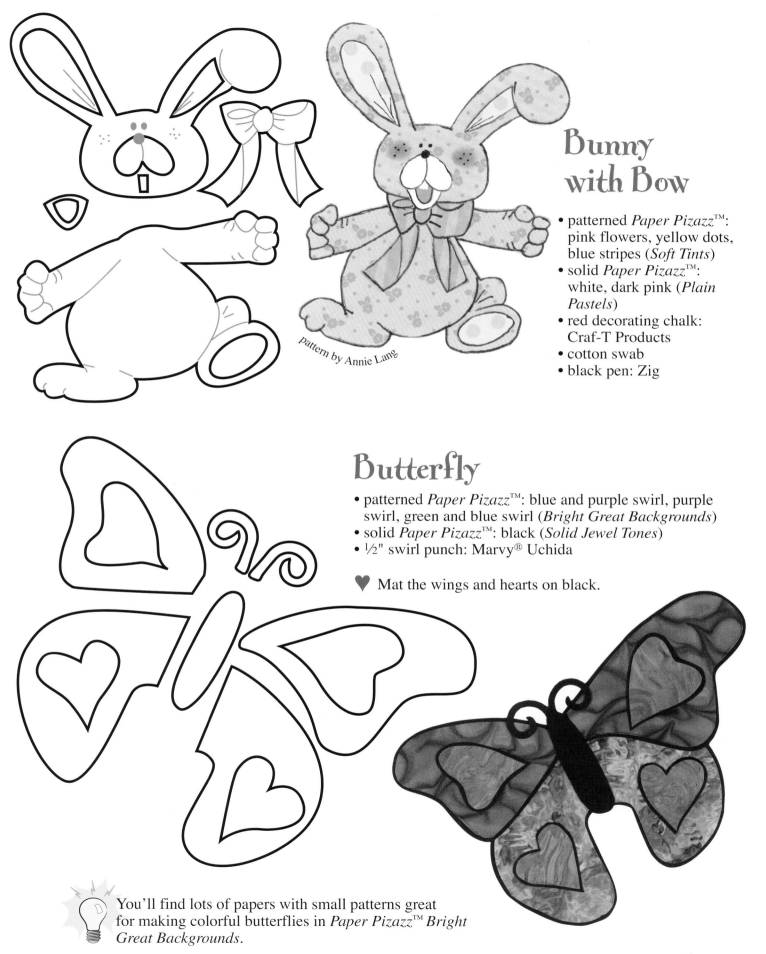

pattern by Annie Lang

Bunny with Bow

- patterned *Paper Pizazz*™: pink flowers, yellow dots, blue stripes (*Soft Tints*)
- solid *Paper Pizazz*™: white, dark pink (*Plain Pastels*)
- red decorating chalk: Craf-T Products
- cotton swab
- black pen: Zig

Butterfly

- patterned *Paper Pizazz*™: blue and purple swirl, purple swirl, green and blue swirl (*Bright Great Backgrounds*)
- solid *Paper Pizazz*™: black (*Solid Jewel Tones*)
- ½" swirl punch: Marvy® Uchida

♥ Mat the wings and hearts on black.

You'll find lots of papers with small patterns great for making colorful butterflies in *Paper Pizazz*™ *Bright Great Backgrounds*.

Birthday Cake

- patterned *Paper Pizazz*™: pink dots (*Lisa Williams Pink, Lavender & Beige*); blue stars (*Lisa Williams Blue, Yellow & Green*); white lace (*Textured Papers*); yellow checks (*Soft Tints*)
- solid *Paper Pizazz*™: white, pink (*Plain Pastels*); vellum (*Vellum Papers*)
- black pen: Zig

♥ Mat each piece on white.

pattern by Annie Lang

For a very pretty look, use a colored vellum sheet (found in *Paper Pizazz*™ *Colored Vellum*) for the frosting.

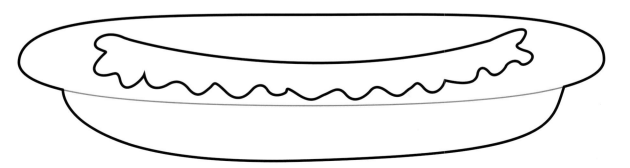

Wedding Cake

- patterned *Paper Pizazz*™: diagonal ribbons* (*Romantic Papers*)
- solid *Paper Pizazz*™: ivory, white (*Plain Pastels*)
- ¼" hole punch: McGill, Inc.
- ⅝" wide cherub punch and 1" wide heart silhouette punch: Marvy® Uchida
- mini scallop scissors: Fiskars
- silver pen: Pentel

Glue an overlapping row of ¼" circle punches to the bottom of each cake tier, then trim it even with the cake edge. Punch out the heart cake topper and trim around the shape with mini-scallop scissors.

cut 3 columns

punch 70 circles

Candy Box

- patterned *Paper Pizazz*™: red roses* (*Blooming Blossoms*); white moiré* (*Wedding*)
- solid *Paper Pizazz*™: white (*Plain Pastels*); black (*Solid Jewel Tones*)
- black pen: Zig
- ♥ Mat bow, ribbon and tag on black.

I Love You

* This paper is also available by the sheet

Candy Canes

- patterned *Paper Pizazz*™: red tartan* (*Christmas*); red stripes (*Coordinating Colors*™ *12"x12" Red & White*)
- solid *Paper Pizazz*™: green (*Solid Jewel Tones*); red (*Plain Brights*); specialty gold* (*Metallic Papers*)
- gold pen: Zebra

♥ Mat bow, berries and leaves on gold.

pine boughs* paper from *Paper Pizazz*™ *Christmas*

* This paper is also available by the sheet

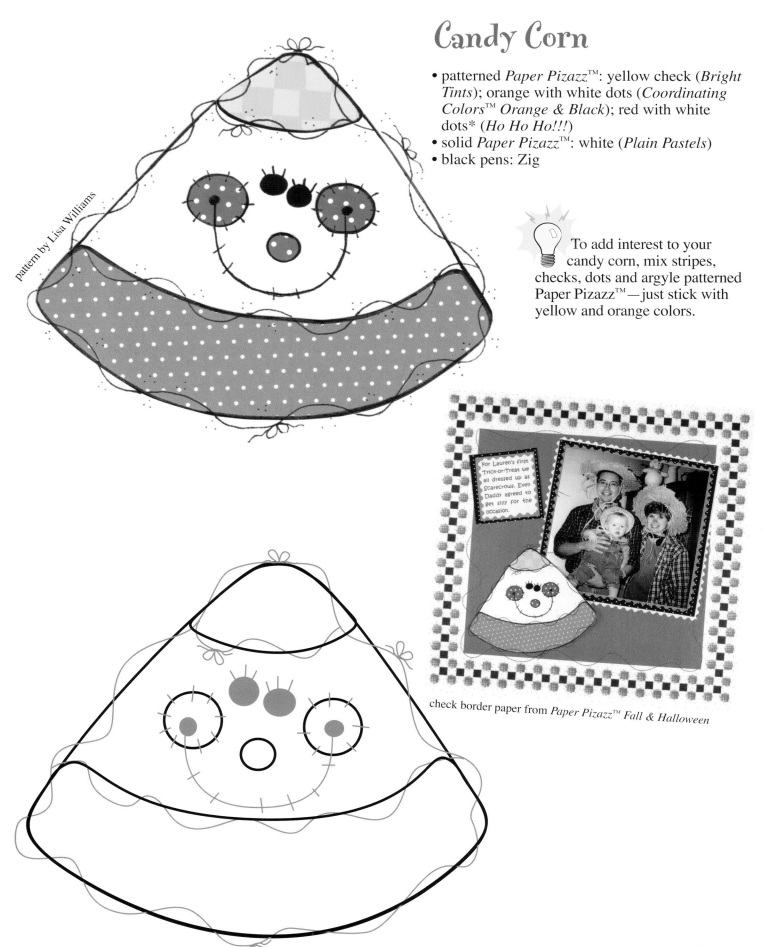

Candy Corn

- patterned *Paper Pizazz*™: yellow check (*Bright Tints*); orange with white dots (*Coordinating Colors*™ *Orange & Black*); red with white dots* (*Ho Ho Ho!!!*)
- solid *Paper Pizazz*™: white (*Plain Pastels*)
- black pens: Zig

pattern by Lisa Williams

To add interest to your candy corn, mix stripes, checks, dots and argyle patterned Paper Pizazz™—just stick with yellow and orange colors.

For Lauren's first Trick-or-Treat we all dressed up as Scarecrows. Even Daddy agreed to get silly for the occasion.

check border paper from *Paper Pizazz*™ *Fall & Halloween*

* This paper is also available by the sheet

Canteen

- patterned *Paper Pizazz*™: red and black plaid* (*The Great Outdoors*); brown crushed suede* (*Black & White Photos*)
- solid *Paper Pizazz*™: gray (*Solid Jewel Tones*)
- black pen: Zig

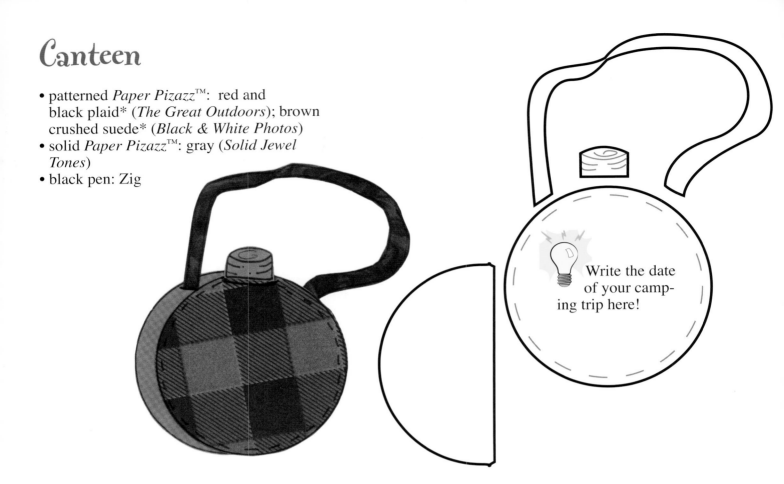

Write the date of your camping trip here!

Car

- patterned *Paper Pizazz*™: denim* (*Country*)
- solid *Paper Pizazz*™: vellum (*Vellum Papers*); white, yellow (*Plain Pastels*); gray, black (*Solid Jewel Tones*)
- black pen: Zig

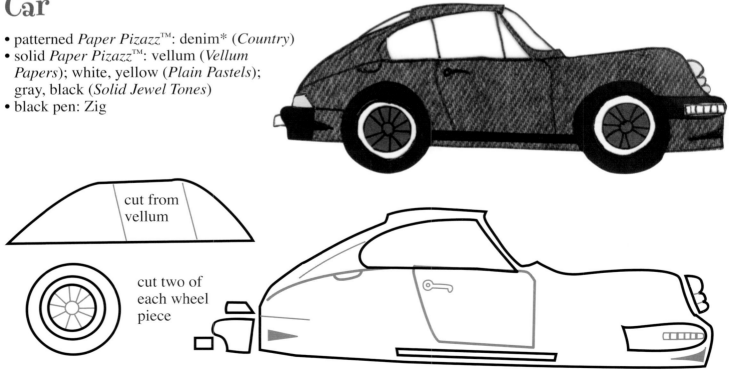

cut from vellum

cut two of each wheel piece

* This paper is also available by the sheet

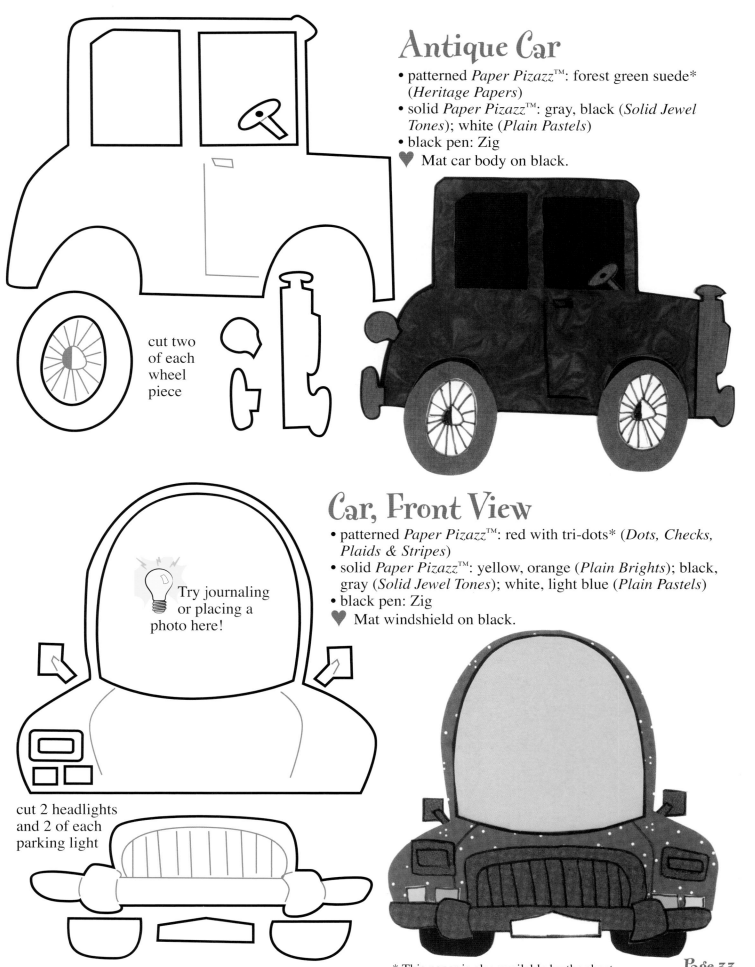

Antique Car

- patterned *Paper Pizazz*™: forest green suede* (*Heritage Papers*)
- solid *Paper Pizazz*™: gray, black (*Solid Jewel Tones*); white (*Plain Pastels*)
- black pen: Zig
- 💜 Mat car body on black.

cut two of each wheel piece

Car, Front View

- patterned *Paper Pizazz*™: red with tri-dots* (*Dots, Checks, Plaids & Stripes*)
- solid *Paper Pizazz*™: yellow, orange (*Plain Brights*); black, gray (*Solid Jewel Tones*); white, light blue (*Plain Pastels*)
- black pen: Zig
- 💜 Mat windshield on black.

Try journaling or placing a photo here!

cut 2 headlights and 2 of each parking light

* This paper is also available by the sheet

Carousel Horse #1

- patterned *Paper Pizazz*™: white moiré* (*Wedding*); red moiré* (*Black & White Photos*); purple moiré* (*Pretty Papers*); gold sponged stars* (*A Woman's Scrapbook*)
- solid *Paper Pizazz*™: specialty gold* (*Metallic Papers*); black (*Solid Jewel Tones*)
- black pen: Zig

♥ Mat each piece on black.

star* paper from *Paper Pizazz*™ *Adult Birthday*

Carousel horses come in all colors. Try some of the papers in *Paper Pizazz*™ *Textured Papers* (see the leather boot on page 23 for an example).

* This paper is also available by the sheet

Carousel Horse #2

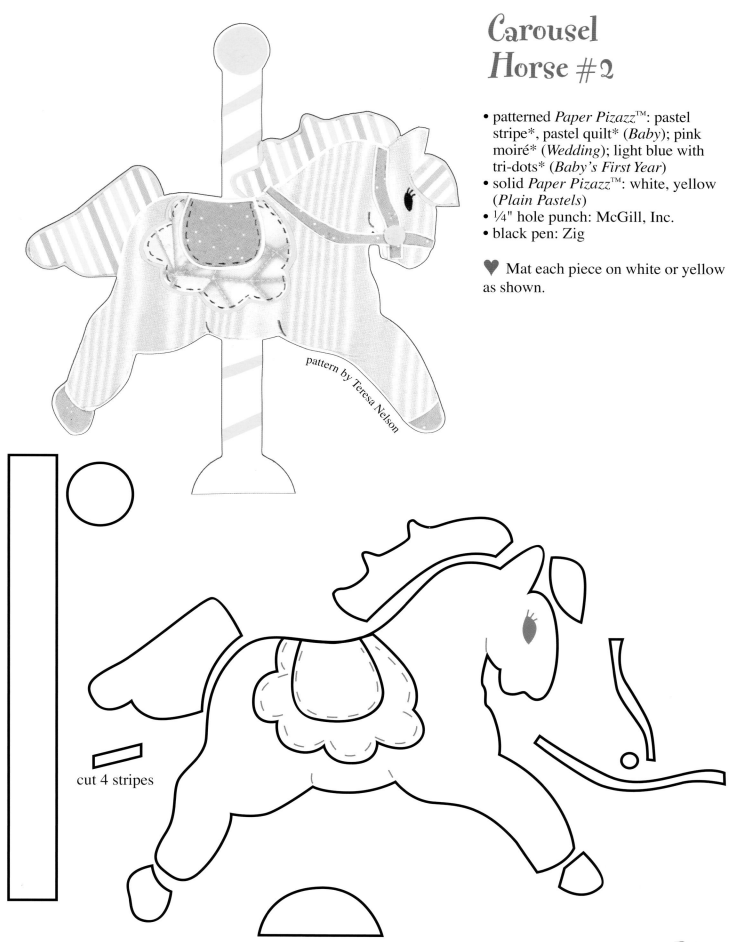

- patterned *Paper Pizazz*™: pastel stripe*, pastel quilt* (*Baby*); pink moiré* (*Wedding*); light blue with tri-dots* (*Baby's First Year*)
- solid *Paper Pizazz*™: white, yellow (*Plain Pastels*)
- ¼" hole punch: McGill, Inc.
- black pen: Zig

♥ Mat each piece on white or yellow as shown.

pattern by Teresa Nelson

cut 4 stripes

Castle

- patterned *Paper Pizazz*™: cobblestones (*Textured Papers*); barnwood* (*Country*); blue and green geometric (*Bright Great Backgrounds*)
- solid *Paper Pizazz*™: black, gray (*Solid Jewel Tones*); green, blue (*Plain Brights*)
- ¼" hole punch: McGill, Inc.
- black pen: Zig

♥ Mat each piece on black.

Silhouette photos of people and place them in the turret above the windows—a great idea for costume parties and plays!

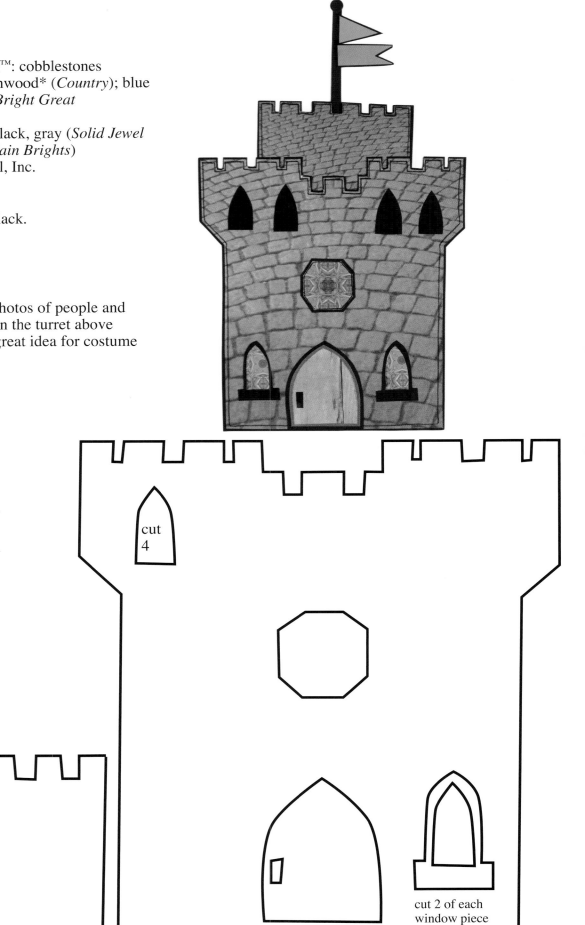

cut 4

cut 2 of each window piece

* This paper is also available by the sheet

Beach Cat

- patterned *Paper Pizazz*™: cheetah (*Wild Things*); oatmeal handmade (*Solid Muted Colors*); black leather (*Textured Papers*); red dots (*Bright Tints*)
- solid *Paper Pizazz*™: blue (*Solid Muted Colors*); black (*Solid Jewel Tones*)
- black pen: Zig
- white pen: Pentel

♥ Mat each piece on black.

pattern by Ruth Ninneman

cut 2 feet

mat on black and glue to umbrella center

Cat with Bow

- patterned *Paper Pizazz*™: pink and peach muted (*Light Great Backgrounds*); yellow check (*Soft Tints*)
- solid *Paper Pizazz*™: white (*Plain Pastels*)
- black pen: Zig
- ♥ Mat each piece on white.

cut 4 paws

pattern by Teresa Nelson

Country Cat

- patterned *Paper Pizazz*™: ivory crackled (*Textured Papers*); navy blue pinstripe, red with stars* (*Dots, Checks, Plaids & Stripes*)
- black pen: Zig

With a change of paper, this can be a spooky Halloween cat.

pattern by Lisa Williams

* This paper is also available by the sheet

Cat with Fish Bowl

- patterned *Paper Pizazz*™: gold sponged stars (*Spattered, Crackled, Sponged*); pool water* (*Vacation #2*); spiral vellum* (*Vellum Papers*)
- solid *Paper Pizazz*™: black (*Solid Jewel Tones*)
- goldfish Punch-Out™: *Paper Pizazz*™ *Clever Frames Punch-Outs*™
- black pen: Zig
  - white pen: Pentel
  - red and green pens: Marvy® Uchida

♥ Mat each piece on black.

Fishing Cat

- patterned *Paper Pizazz*™: woven fabric (*Textured Papers*)
- solid *Paper Pizazz*™: dark pink, ivory, aqua (*Plain Pastels*)
- ¼" hole punch: McGill, Inc.
- black pen: Zig

🖤 Mat each piece on ivory or aqua as shown.

pattern by Nance Wilhite-Kueneman

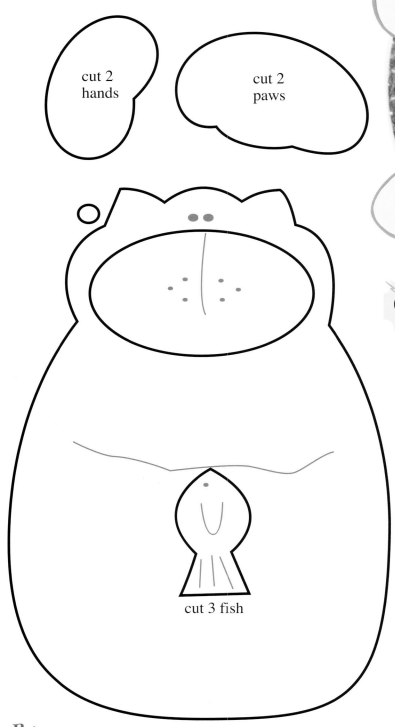

cut 2 hands

cut 2 paws

cut 3 fish

Use embroidery floss or yarn instead of a pen to make the fishing line.

argyle* paper from *Paper Pizazz*™ *Dots, Checks Plaids & Stripes*

* This paper is also available by the sheet

Scary Cat

- patterned *Paper Pizazz*™: black with white dots* (*Coordinating Colors*™ *Orange & Black*)
- solid *Paper Pizazz*™: gray (*Solid Jewel tones*); red (*Plain Brights*)
- red decorating chalk: Craf-T Products
- cotton swab
- black pen: Zig

Pattern by Lisa Williams

Use orange with white dots paper to make a scary tabby cat. A few scary cats perched on a picket fence would make a fun Halloween border.

Champagne Bottle

- patterned *Paper Pizazz*™: green with dots vellum (*Colored Vellum*); small bubbles* (*Baby*); cork board* (*School Days*)
- solid *Paper Pizazz*™: specialty gold* (*Metallic Papers*); white (*Plain Pastels*); black, dark green (*Solid Jewel Tones*)
- black pen: Zig

♥ Mat each piece on black.
★ Mat the finished piece on green.

Write a wedding date or "Happy Anniversary" on the bottle's label.

Glue the vellum to the bubbles paper, then trace and cut out the champagne bottle.

2001

* This paper is also available by the sheet

Children of the World

- patterned *Paper Pizazz*™: pool water* (*Vacation #2*); green marble* (*Black & White Photos*); denim* (*Country*); purple swirl, green swirl, bright bubbles, purple and green swirl (*Bright Great Backgrounds*)
- solid *Paper Pizazz*™: ivory, tan, white, yellow (*Plain Pastels*); black, brown (*Solid Jewel Tones*); medium brown (*Solid Muted Colors*); red (*Solid Brights*)
- pink and red decorating chalk: Craf-T Products
- cotton swab
- black pen: Zig

♥ Mat banner on black.

This pattern has endless possibilities. Use it for pages about classroom activities and environmental themes. Or write "Peace on Earth" on the banner for your holiday pages or a special card.

cut 4

cut 4

cut 4

cut 4

All the little Children of the World

* This paper is also available by the sheet

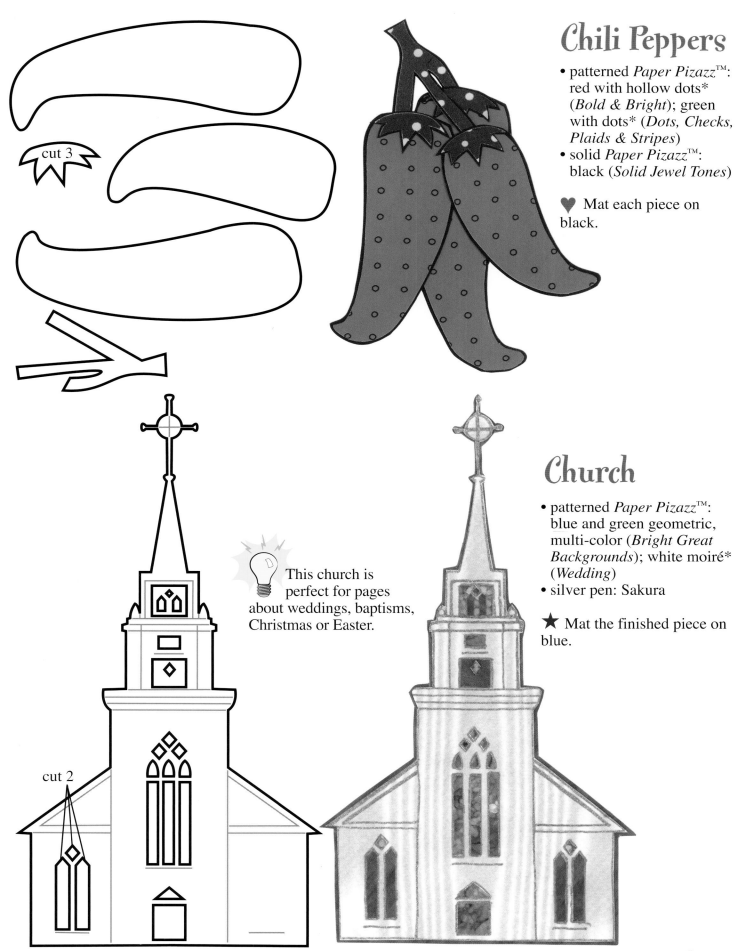

Chili Peppers

- patterned *Paper Pizazz*™: red with hollow dots* (*Bold & Bright*); green with dots* (*Dots, Checks, Plaids & Stripes*)
- solid *Paper Pizazz*™: black (*Solid Jewel Tones*)

♥ Mat each piece on black.

cut 3

Church

- patterned *Paper Pizazz*™: blue and green geometric, multi-color (*Bright Great Backgrounds*); white moiré* (*Wedding*)
- silver pen: Sakura

★ Mat the finished piece on blue.

This church is perfect for pages about weddings, baptisms, Christmas or Easter.

cut 2

* This paper is also available by the sheet

Clown in a Flower Pot

- patterned *Paper Pizazz*™: purple with dots* (*Child's Play*); red moiré* (*Black & White Photos*)
- solid *Paper Pizazz*™: white (*Plain Pastels*); yellow (*Solid Muted Colors*); black (*Solid Jewel Tones*)
- black pen: Zig

♥ Mat each piece on black.

pattern by Teresa Nelson

cut 2 arms

cut 2 cuffs

cut 2 hands

* This paper is also available by the sheet

Computer

- patterned *Paper Pizazz*™: white moiré* (*Wedding*); aqua stars (*Bright Great Backgrounds*)
- solid *Paper Pizazz*™: white (*Plain Pastels*); black (*Solid Jewel Tones*)
- black pen: Zig

Write a note in the screen.

♥ Mat each piece on black.

Cookie Jar

- patterned *Paper Pizazz*™: chocolate chip cookies* (*Child's Play*); vellum with dots* (*Vellum Papers*)
- solid *Paper Pizazz*™: black (*Solid Jewel Tones*)
- black pen: Zig

♥ Mat each piece on black.

cookies

Trim cookies from chocolate chip cookies paper and let them peek from the top of the jar. This pattern works well with candy or jelly beans paper, too (see the *Paper Pizazz*™ *Yummy Papers* book).

cookies

* This paper is also available by the sheet

Country Valentine Couple

- patterned *Paper Pizazz*™: green and yellow plaid (*Jewel Plaids*); burgundy with tri-dots* (*Dots, Checks, Plaids & Stripes*); denim* (*Country*); burgundy suede* (*Heritage Papers*)
- solid *Paper Pizazz*™: tan (*Plain Pastels*); yellow, mauve, light brown, medium brown, dark brown (*Solid Muted Colors*); black, blue (*Solid Jewel Tones*)
- pink and brown decorating chalk: Craf-T Products
- cotton swab
- black pen: Zig

Apply decorating chalk to the sides of the bag (see page 7 for instructions) to add dimension and depth.

pattern by Temple Garman

insert overalls, stick and hand

Be mine

* This paper is also available by the sheet

Cow

- patterned *Paper Pizazz*™: peach with tri-dots* (*Light Great Backgrounds*); black with white dots* (*Coordinating Colors*™ *Orange & Black*)
- solid *Paper Pizazz*™: white (*Plain Pastels*)
- ¼" hole punch: McGill, Inc.
- black pen: Zig
- white pen: Pentel

♥ Mat each piece on black.

pattern by Teresa Nelson

Use this cow with the moon on page 91 for a nursery rhyme page.

cut 2 nostrils

cut 4 hooves

Cross

- patterned *Paper Pizazz*™: blue swirl*, green swirl* (*Pretty Papers*)
- solid *Paper Pizazz*™: specialty gold* (*Metallic Papers*); black (*Solid Jewel Tones*)

♥ Mat each piece on black.

Cut a half circle from each swirl pattern, cut in half and glue behind the cross as shown.

Crown

- patterned *Paper Pizazz*™: gold leaf (*Textured Papers*); white moiré*, purple satin* (*Wedding*); burgundy*, forest green suede* (*Heritage Papers*)
- solid *Paper Pizazz*™: black (*Solid Jewel Tones*)
- black pen: Zig

♥ Mat each piece on black.

★ Mat the finished piece on black.

* This paper is also available by the sheet

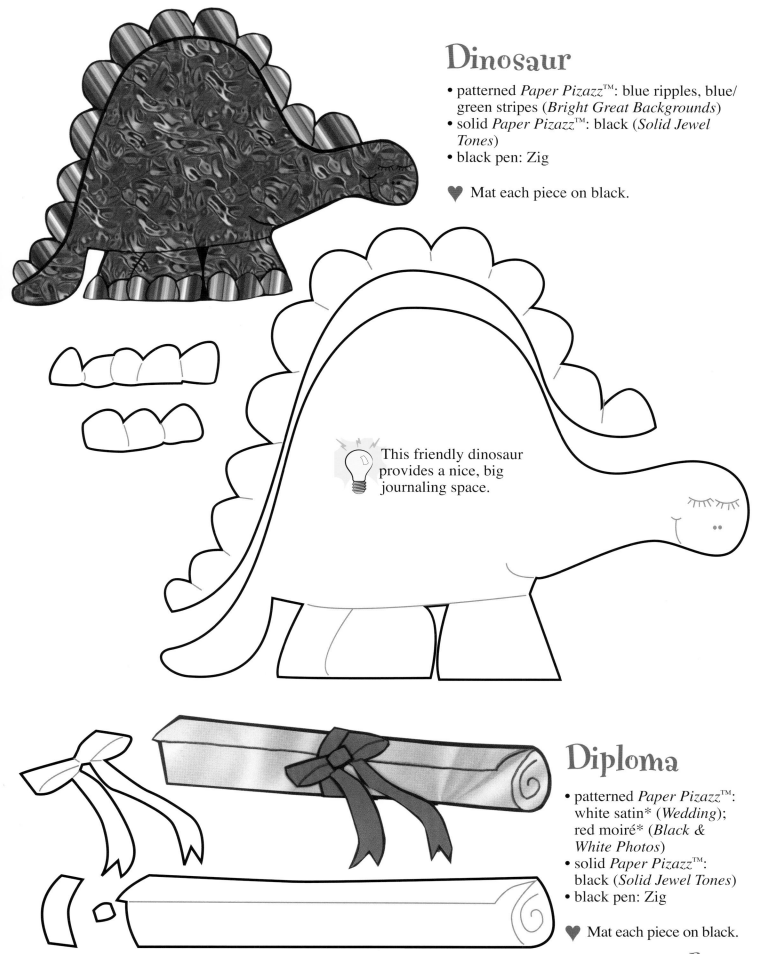

Dinosaur

- patterned *Paper Pizazz*™: blue ripples, blue/green stripes (*Bright Great Backgrounds*)
- solid *Paper Pizazz*™: black (*Solid Jewel Tones*)
- black pen: Zig

♥ Mat each piece on black.

This friendly dinosaur provides a nice, big journaling space.

Diploma

- patterned *Paper Pizazz*™: white satin* (*Wedding*); red moiré* (*Black & White Photos*)
- solid *Paper Pizazz*™: black (*Solid Jewel Tones*)
- black pen: Zig

♥ Mat each piece on black.

* This paper is also available by the sheet

Disney: Snow White

- solid *Paper Pizazz*™: yellow, red (*Plain Brights*); black, dark blue, (*Solid Jewel Tones*); medium blue, white (*Plain Pastels*); peach (*Solid Muted Colors*)
- black, pink, blue and brown pens: Zig
- white pen: Pentel
- rose decorating chalk: Craf-T Products
- cotton swab

♥ Mat each piece on black.

insert head

insert shoulders

cut sleeve lining in red and glue behind outer sleeves

Disney: Cinderella

- solid *Paper Pizazz*™: yellow (*Plain Brights*); light blue, medium blue, tan, white (*Plain Pastels*)
- black pen: Zig
- white pen: Pentel
- pink and blue colored pencils

insert slip

Disney: Ariel

- solid *Paper Pizazz*™: peach (*Solid Muted Colors*); lavender, mint green (*Plain Pastels*); red, green (*Plain Brights*); black (*Solid Jewel Tones*)
- rose and black pens: Zig
- white and blue pens: Pentel

♥ Mat each piece on black.

insert head

Disney: Tinker Bell

- solid *Paper Pizazz*™: yellow, ivory, blue, white (*Plain Pastels*); lime green (*Plain Brights*); gray-blue (*Solid Muted Colors*)
- blue colored pencil: EK Success
- black and red pens: Zig
- white pen: Pentel

♥ Mat each piece on black.

Disney: Dumbo

- solid *Paper Pizazz*™: black, gray (*Solid Jewel Tones*); goldenrod, red, blue (*Plain Brights*); mauve (*Solid Jewel Tones*); peach, white (*Plain Pastels*)
- black pen: Zig

♥ Mat each piece on black.

Disney: Mickey Mouse

- solid *Paper Pizazz*™: black (*Solid Jewel Tones*); red (*Plain Brights*); yellow (*Solid Muted Colors*); white (*Plain Pastels*)
- black and red pens: Zig
- white pen: Pentel

♥ Mat each piece on black.

Disney: Minnie Mouse

- solid *Paper Pizazz*™: yellow, light mauve, dark mauve (*Solid Muted Colors*); white (*Plain Pastels*); black (*Solid Jewel Tones*)
- black and red pens: Zig
- white pen: Pentel

♥ Mat each piece on black.

Disney: Eeyore

- solid *Paper Pizazz*™: peach (*Solid Muted Colors*); blue, lavender, pink, white (*Plain Pastels*); black, gray (*Solid Jewel Tones*)
- black pen: Zig

★ Mat the finished piece on black.

Disney: Winnie the Pooh

- solid *Paper Pizazz*™: red, goldenrod (*Plain Brights*); black (*Solid Jewel Tones*)
- black and red pens: Zig

♥ Mat each piece on black.

Disney: Jessie

- solid *Paper Pizazz*™: blue (*Plain Brights*); ivory (*Plain Pastels*); yellow, peach, red-brown (*Solid Muted Colors*); specialty gold* (*Metallic Papers*); red, black (*Solid Jewel Tones*)
- black, red and green pens: Zig
- silver and white pens: Pentel

* This paper is also available by the sheet

Disney: Woody

- solid *Paper Pizazz*™: yellow, blue, red (*Plain Brights*); peach, brown, red-brown (*Solid Muted Colors*); specialty gold* (*Metallic Papers*); dark brown, black (*Solid Jewel Tones*); white (*Plain Pastels*)
- black and red pens: Zig
- white and silver pens: Pentel

* This paper is also available by the sheet

Dog with Bone

- patterned *Paper Pizazz*™: gold leaf (*Textured Papers*); ivory sponged (*Spattered, Crackled, Sponged*)
- solid *Paper Pizazz*™: black (*Solid Jewel Tones*)
- black pen: Zig
- white pen: Pentel

♥ Mat each piece on black.

Change this dog's color to match your favorite pooch! Try the brown crushed suede Paper Pizazz™ on page 18 for another nice look.

Dog with Spots

- patterned *Paper Pizazz*™: gold sponged stars* (*Spattered, Crackled, Sponged*); brown crushed suede* (*Black & White Photos*)
- solid *Paper Pizazz*™: pink (*Plain Pastels*); red (*Plain Brights*); black (*Solid Jewel Tones*)
- black pen: Zig
- white pen: Pentel

pattern by Teresa Nelson

Dove with Olive Branch

- patterned *Paper Pizazz*™: white moiré* (*Wedding*); forest green suede* (*Heritage Papers*); blue swirl* (*Pretty Papers*)
- solid *Paper Pizazz*™: black (*Solid Jewel Tones*); specialty gold* (*Metallic Papers*)
- black pen: Zig

♥ Mat the blue swirl circle on gold and glue it to the black circle. Mat the other pieces on black.

* This paper is also available by the sheet

Dragon

- patterned *Paper Pizazz*™: forest green suede (*Heritage Papers*); blue and green tiles (*Bright Great Backgrounds*)
- solid *Paper Pizazz*™: purple (*Solid Muted Colors*); vellum (*Vellum Papers*)
- black pen: Zig
- white and aqua pens: Pentel

Of course, dragons come in all colors!

cut 2 horns

cut 18 claws

glue tail here

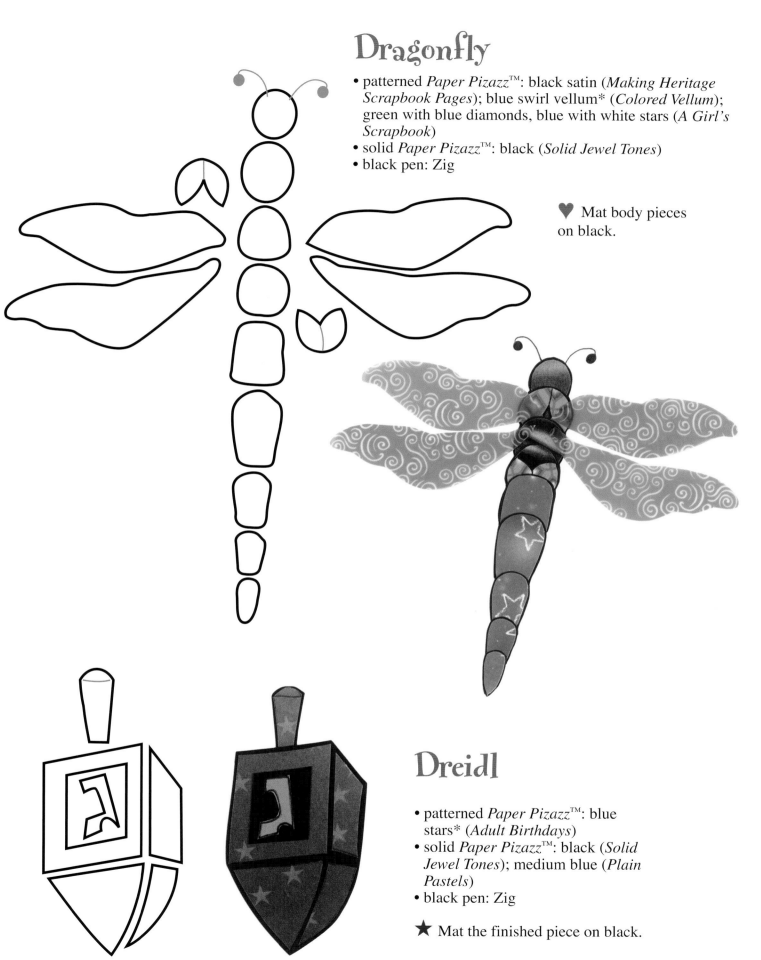

Dragonfly

- patterned *Paper Pizazz*™: black satin (*Making Heritage Scrapbook Pages*); blue swirl vellum* (*Colored Vellum*); green with blue diamonds, blue with white stars (*A Girl's Scrapbook*)
- solid *Paper Pizazz*™: black (*Solid Jewel Tones*)
- black pen: Zig

♥ Mat body pieces on black.

Dreidl

- patterned *Paper Pizazz*™: blue stars* (*Adult Birthdays*)
- solid *Paper Pizazz*™: black (*Solid Jewel Tones*); medium blue (*Plain Pastels*)
- black pen: Zig

★ Mat the finished piece on black.

* This paper is also available by the sheet

Duck in Half Egg

- patterned *Paper Pizazz*™: pink checks, blue dots (*Soft Tints*)
- solid *Paper Pizazz*™: yellow, orange, green, white (*Solid Pastels*)
- ½" flower punch: Family Treasures
- ¼" hole punch: McGill, Inc.
- black pen: Zig

Use the half egg pattern to make a pocket for Easter mementos.

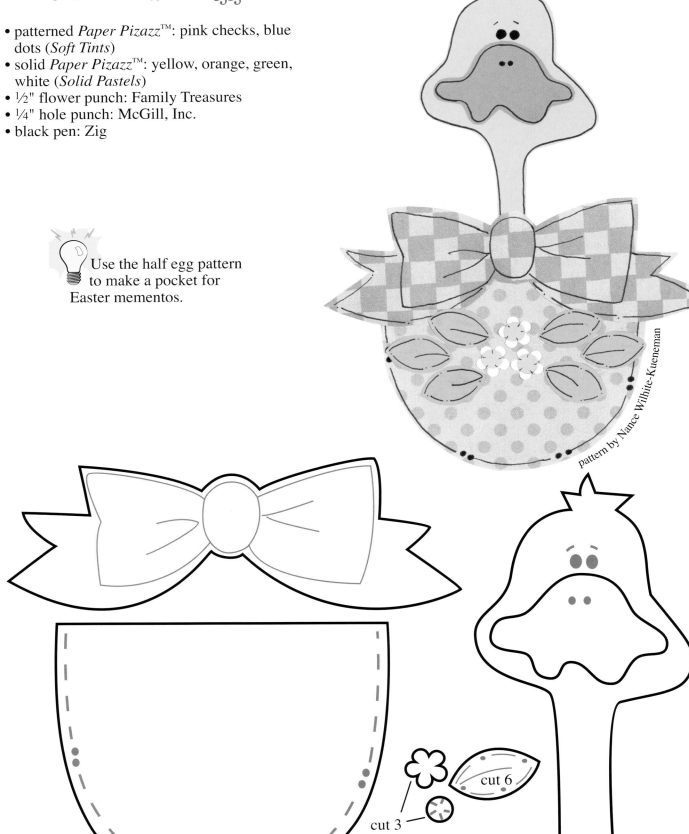

pattern by Nance Wilhite-Kueneman

cut 6

cut 3

Duck with Blue Bow

- patterned *Paper Pizazz*™: yellow dots, yellow check, blue stripe (*Soft Tints*)
- solid *Paper Pizazz*™: white, orange (*Plain Pastels*)
- ⅜" hole punch: McGill, Inc.
- black pen: Zig

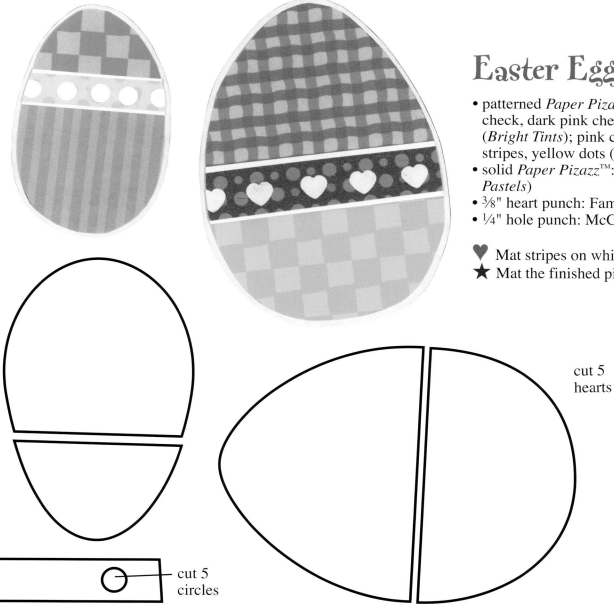

Easter Eggs

- patterned *Paper Pizazz*™: yellow check, dark pink check, blue dots (*Bright Tints*); pink check, blue stripes, yellow dots (*Soft Tints*)
- solid *Paper Pizazz*™: white (*Plain Pastels*)
- ⅜" heart punch: Family Treasures
- ¼" hole punch: McGill, Inc.

♥ Mat stripes on white.
★ Mat the finished piece on white.

cut 5 hearts

cut 5 circles

Elephant with Balloon

- patterned *Paper Pizazz*™: blue stripes, blue dots, yellow dots, green plaid, pink check (*Soft Tints*)
- solid *Paper Pizazz*™: white (*Plain Pastels*)
- black pen: Zig

♥ Mat each piece on white.

green stripe and purple dot papers from *Paper Pizazz*™ *Soft Tints*

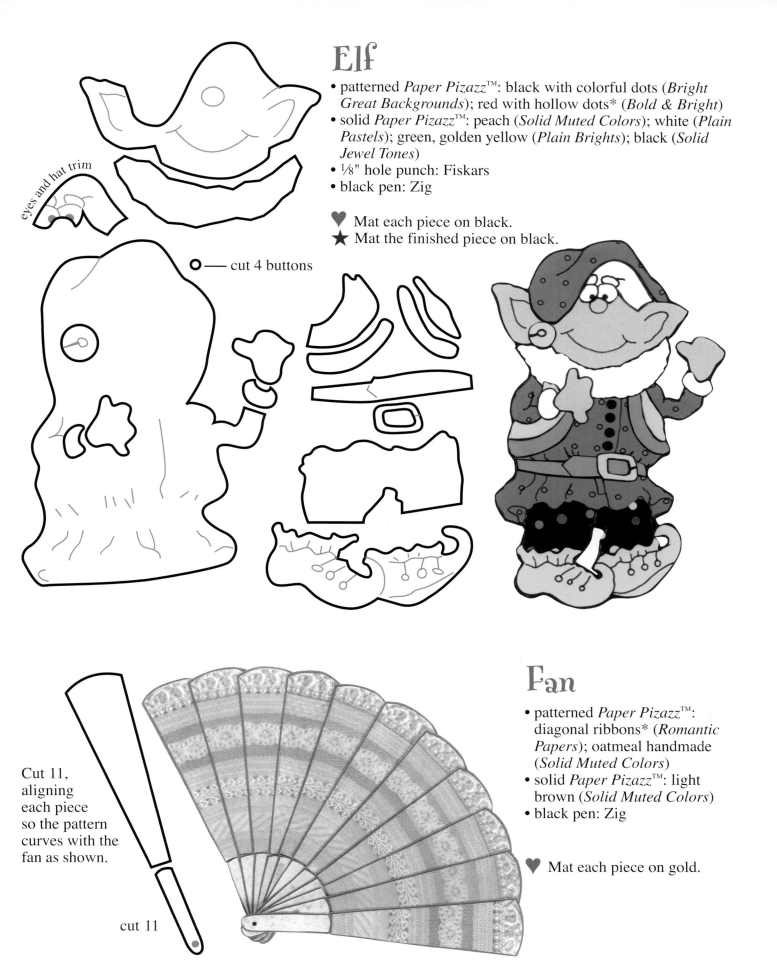

Elf

- patterned *Paper Pizazz*™: black with colorful dots (*Bright Great Backgrounds*); red with hollow dots* (*Bold & Bright*)
- solid *Paper Pizazz*™: peach (*Solid Muted Colors*); white (*Plain Pastels*); green, golden yellow (*Plain Brights*); black (*Solid Jewel Tones*)
- ⅛" hole punch: Fiskars
- black pen: Zig

♥ Mat each piece on black.
★ Mat the finished piece on black.

eyes and hat trim

○ — cut 4 buttons

Fan

- patterned *Paper Pizazz*™: diagonal ribbons* (*Romantic Papers*); oatmeal handmade (*Solid Muted Colors*)
- solid *Paper Pizazz*™: light brown (*Solid Muted Colors*)
- black pen: Zig

♥ Mat each piece on gold.

Cut 11, aligning each piece so the pattern curves with the fan as shown.

cut 11

* This paper is also available by the sheet

Firecrackers

- patterned *Paper Pizazz*™: red with stars* (*Dots, Checks, Plaids & Stripes*); blue stars* (*Adult Birthdays*)
- solid *Paper Pizazz*™: navy blue, black (*Solid Jewel Tones*); yellow (*Plain Brights*)
- ½" and ¼" star punches: Family Treasures
- red and black pens: Zig

♥ Mat each piece on black.

 Use a glitter pen to make festive fireworks sparkles on your page.

cut 10 small stars

* This paper is also available by the sheet

Christmas Fireplace

- patterned *Paper Pizazz*™: brick wall*, barnwood* (*Country*); autumn leaves* (*Holidays & Seasons*); red with white dots*, green plaid* (*Ho, Ho, Ho!!!*); green with white dots*, red tartan* (*Christmas*)
- solid *Paper Pizazz*™: white (*Plain Pastels*); black (*Solid Jewel Tones*)
- black pen: Zig

♥ Mat each piece on black.

cut 1 for the mantel and 1 for the hearth

Widen the fireplace and add stockings for additional family members. Write their names on the cuffs.

cut 2

cut 2 of each stocking piece

cut 11 bricks

pattern by Diane Bliss

Fish

- patterned *Paper Pizazz*™: tortoise shell, turquoise suede, green and blue swirl (*Bright Great Backgrounds*)
- solid *Paper Pizazz*™: brown, black (*Solid Jewel Tones*)
- ¼" hole punch: McGill, Inc.
- yellow and purple decorating chalk: Craf-T Products
- cotton swab
- black pen: Zig
- white pen: Pentel

★ Mat the finished piece on black.

Colorful Fish

- patterned *Paper Pizazz*™: blue multi-colored, blue textured, blue and green geometric (*Bright Great Backgrounds*)
- solid *Paper Pizazz*™: yellow (*Solid Muted Colors*)
- black pen: Zig

♥ Mat each piece on black.
★ Mat the finished piece on yellow.

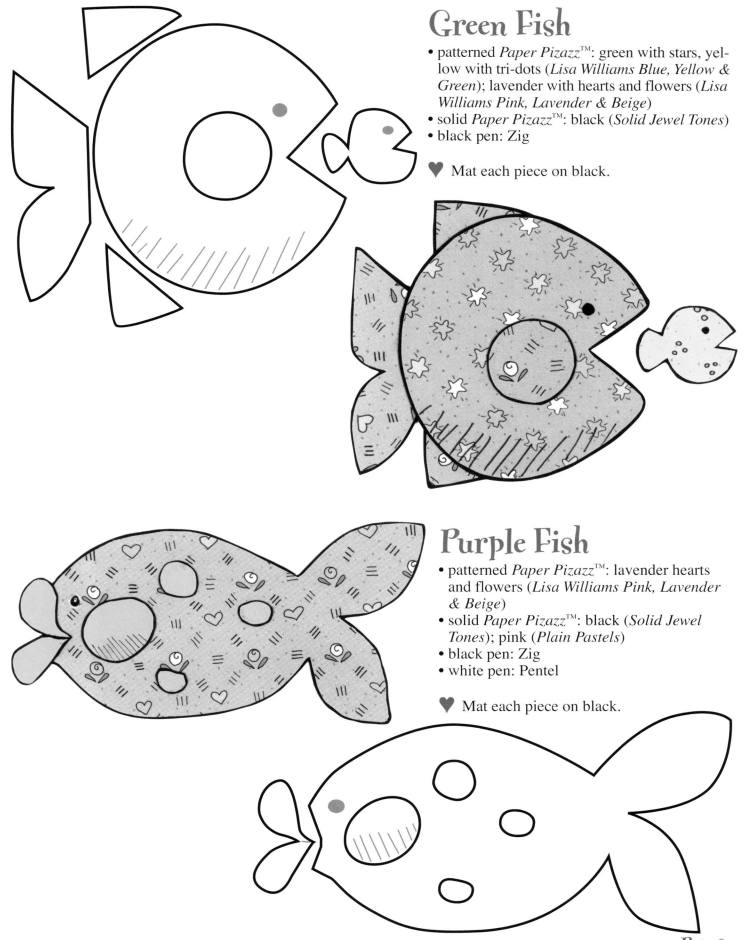

Green Fish

- patterned *Paper Pizazz*™: green with stars, yellow with tri-dots (*Lisa Williams Blue, Yellow & Green*); lavender with hearts and flowers (*Lisa Williams Pink, Lavender & Beige*)
- solid *Paper Pizazz*™: black (*Solid Jewel Tones*)
- black pen: Zig

♥ Mat each piece on black.

Purple Fish

- patterned *Paper Pizazz*™: lavender hearts and flowers (*Lisa Williams Pink, Lavender & Beige*)
- solid *Paper Pizazz*™: black (*Solid Jewel Tones*); pink (*Plain Pastels*)
- black pen: Zig
- white pen: Pentel

♥ Mat each piece on black.

Flower Bouquet

- patterned *Paper Pizazz*™: muted roses* (*Wedding*); purple mottled (*Bright Great Backgrounds*); purple moiré* (*Pretty Papers*)
- solid *Paper Pizazz*™: yellow (*Solid Muted Colors*); white (*Plain Pastels*)
- green and silver pens: Zig

cut 2

cut 3

Flowers, Country

- patterned *Paper Pizazz*™: burgundy with tri-dots* (*Dots, Checks, Plaids & Stripes*); forest green suede* (*Heritage Papers*); yellow plaid (*Jewel Plaids*)
- black pen: Zig

patterns by Temple Garman

cut 3

cut 2

cut 2

cut 2

* This paper is also available by the sheet

Football Helmet

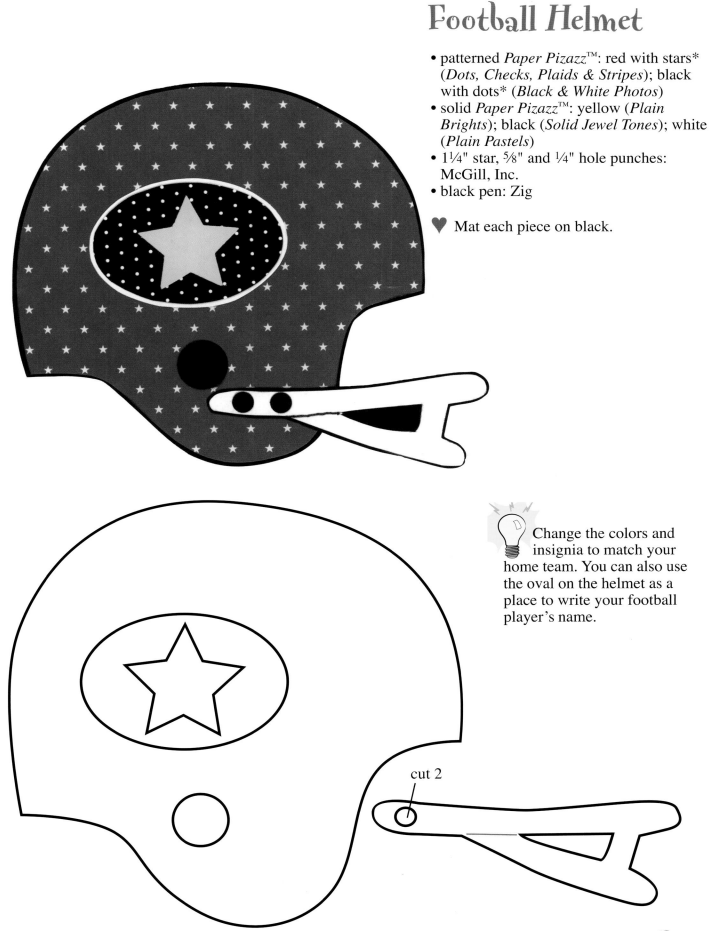

- patterned *Paper Pizazz*™: red with stars*
  (*Dots, Checks, Plaids & Stripes*); black
  with dots* (*Black & White Photos*)
- solid *Paper Pizazz*™: yellow (*Plain
  Brights*); black (*Solid Jewel Tones*); white
  (*Plain Pastels*)
- 1¼" star, ⅝" and ¼" hole punches:
  McGill, Inc.
- black pen: Zig

♥ Mat each piece on black.

Change the colors and
insignia to match your
home team. You can also use
the oval on the helmet as a
place to write your football
player's name.

cut 2

* This paper is also available by the sheet

Frankenstein

- patterned *Paper Pizazz*™: yellow and black check* (*Bold & Bright*); red with white dots* (*Ho, Ho, Ho!!!*)
- solid *Paper Pizazz*™: lime green, orange (*Solid Brights*); black (*Solid Jewel Tones*); white (*Plain Pastels*)
- ¼" hole punch: McGill, Inc.
- white pen: Pentel
- black pen: Zig

pattern by Lisa Williams

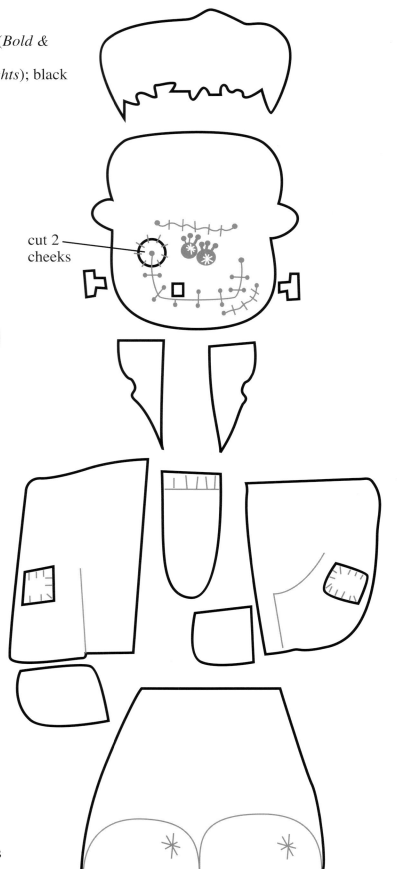

cut 2 cheeks

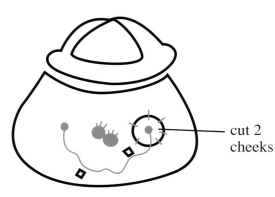

cut 2 cheeks

* This paper is also available by the sheet

Frog

- patterned *Paper Pizazz*™: green check (*Bright Tints*); barnwood* (*Country*)
- solid *Paper Pizazz*™: white, yellow (*Plain Pastels*); black, red, dark green (*Solid Jewel Tones*)
- black pen: Zig
- ♥ Mat each piece on black.

pattern by Annie Lang

Ghost

- solid *Paper Pizazz*™: vellum (*Vellum Papers*); white (*Plain Pastels*)
- black pen: Zig

Cut the ghost's body from vellum and the other pieces from white.

* This paper is also available by the sheet

Gingerbread Boy & Girl

- patterned *Paper Pizazz*™: golden brown crushed suede (*Making Heritage Scrapbook Pages*); red and green dots* (*Ho, Ho, Ho!!!*)
- solid *Paper Pizazz*™: red (*Plain Brights*); white, pink (*Plain Pastels*); black (*Solid Jewel Tones*)
- 7⁄16" heart punch: Marvy® Uchida
- 1⁄8" circle punch: Fiskars
- black pen: Zig

cut 2 eyes and 2 cheeks

cut 3 buttons

cut 8

Giraffe

- patterned *Paper Pizazz*™: yellow dots (*Soft Tints*); brown crushed suede* (*Black & White Photos*)
- black pen: Zig

To save time on the spots, first glue on punched circles, then trim them even with the giraffe.

Pattern by Kathy Christenson

* This paper is also available by the sheet

School Girl

- patterned *Paper Pizazz*™: barnwood* (Country); (*Birthday*); school tartan* (*School Days*)
- solid *Paper Pizazz*™: red, yellow (*Plain Brights*); tan, white, pink (*Plain Pastels*); black (*Solid Jewel Tones*)
- white pen: Pentel
- black pen: Zig

cut 2 cheeks

Cut the back of her hair from yellow and glue behind her head.

A

pattern by Ruth Ninneman

Golf Bag

- patterned *Paper Pizazz*™: leather (*Textured Papers*); forest green suede* (*Heritage Papers*)
- solid *Paper Pizazz*™: black, gray (*Solid Jewel Tones*)
- black pen: Zig

* This paper is also available by the sheet

Hamburger

- patterned *Paper Pizazz*™: brown velvet (*"Velvet" Backgrounds*); yellow checks, green dots (*Bright Tints*); red with white dots * (*Ho, Ho, Ho!!!*); mottled brown with angled border (*Wild Things*)
- solid *Paper Pizazz*™: black (*Solid Jewel Tones*); bright green (*Plain Brights*); tan (*Plain Pastels*)
- teardrop punch: Family Treasures
- black pen: Zig

♥ Mat each piece on black.

This burger is fun to do with a bite out of it! After piecing it, use this pattern to trace and cut out the bite.

cut 13
sesame seeds

    * This paper is also available by the sheet

Happy Spring Banner

- patterned *Paper Pizazz*™: pink check, blue dots (*Soft Tints*)
- solid *Paper Pizazz*™: yellow, white (*Solid Pastels*)
- ½" flower punch: Family Treasures
- ¼" hole punch: McGill, Inc.
- black pen: Zig

pattern by Nance Wilhite-Kueneman

cut 4

Hat Box

- patterned *Paper Pizazz*™: pink moiré* (*Wedding*); laser lace*; roses with stripes (*Romantic Papers*)
- solid *Paper Pizazz*™: white (*Plain Pastels*)

♥ Mat each piece (except the laser lace) on white.

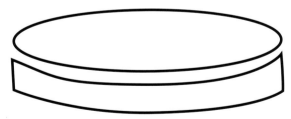

Cut around the bottom edge of the laser lace. Glue the lace to the top half of the box and trim the edges even. Glue the lid to the top of the box over the lace.

* This paper is also available by the sheet

Cowboy Hat

- patterned *Paper Pizazz*™: elephant skin (*Wild Things*)
- solid *Paper Pizazz*™: black (*Solid Jewel Tones*)
- black pen: Zig

♥ Mat each piece on black.

Victorian Hat

- patterned *Paper Pizazz*™: pink moiré* (*Wedding*); laser lace*, roses with stripes (*Romantic Papers*); green, yellow and pink plaid* (*Pastel Plaids*)
- solid *Paper Pizazz*™: white (*Plain Pastels*)
- black pen: Zig

♥ Mat the hat on white.

The roses around the hat crown are cut from patterned paper. Use a different sheet for another look.

* This paper is also available by the sheet

Quilted Heart

- patterned *Paper Pizazz*™: pink stars (*Lisa Williams Pink, Lavender & Beige*); blue stripe, green floral, yellow checks, yellow dots (*Lisa Williams Blue, Yellow & Green*)
- solid *Paper Pizazz*™: white (*Plain Pastels*); black (*Solid Jewel Tones*)
- long scallop scissors: Fiskars
- black pen: Zig

★ Mat the finished piece on black.

Piece the heart on white paper, then trim around it with scallop-edged scissors. Add a black dot to each scallop. Try enlarging this pattern and using photos for the patches instead of paper.

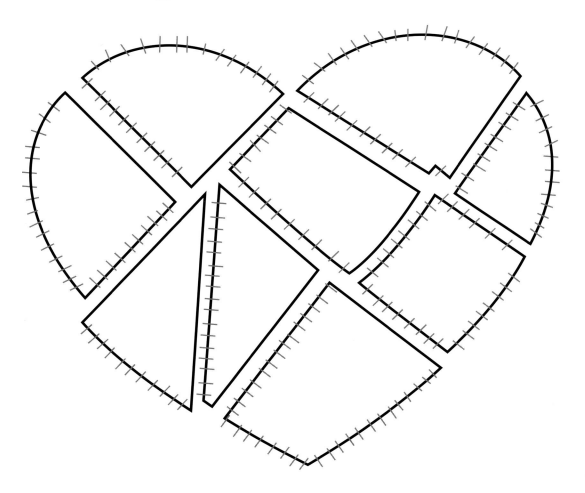

Red, White & Blue Heart

- patterned *Paper Pizazz*™: red and white stripe* (*Ho, Ho, Ho!!!*)
- solid *Paper Pizazz*™: white (*Plain Pastels*); navy blue (*Solid Jewel Tones*)
- long ripple scissors: Fiskars
- 1⅜" star punch: Marvy® Uchida
- black pen: Zig
- white pen: Pentel

This heart was trimmed with ripple scissors, but you can use any pattern-edged or straight scissors.

Helicopter

- patterned *Paper Pizazz*™: vellum swirl* (*Vellum Papers*); colorful stripes* (*Birthday*); green with white dots* (*Christmas*); yellow diamonds (*Bright Tints*)
- solid *Paper Pizazz*™: black (*Solid Jewel Tones*); aqua, red (*Plain Brights*)
- black pen: Zig

♥ Mat each piece on black.

The pattern pieces are on page 81.

Place a photo in the window, and for an interactive layout, attach the tail propeller with a brass paper brad to allow it to spin.

* This paper is also available by the sheet

Helicopter (cont'd)

Ice Cream Cone

Add more scoops for a triple-decker. Use photos as scoops!

- patterned *Paper Pizazz*™: brown plaid (*Coordinating Colors*™ *Flannel Plaids*); chocolate chips* (*Yummy Papers*)
- solid *Paper Pizazz*™: black (*Solid Jewel Tones*)
- black pen: Zig

♥ Mat each piece on black.

* This paper is also available by the sheet

Ice Cream Sundae

- patterned *Paper Pizazz™*: blue diamonds (*Soft Tints*); red and white stripe* (*Ho, Ho, Ho!!!*); brown sponged, pink sponged, red sponged, white speckle (*Bj's Handpainted Papers*); dark brown sponged (*Spattered, Crackled, Sponged*)
- solid *Paper Pizazz™*: vellum (*Vellum Papers*)
- black pen: Zig

♥ Mat each piece on black.

For each sundae glass piece, glue vellum to patterned paper, then trace and cut the pattern piece.

* This paper is also available by the sheet

In-line Skate

- patterned *Paper Pizazz*™: purple with orange hollow dots* (*A Girl's Scrapbook*)
- solid *Paper Pizazz*™: red, yellow, green (*Plain Brights*); orange, black (*Solid Jewel Tones*)
- black pen: Zig

♥ Mat each piece on black.

purple dots and colorful argyle papers from *Paper Pizazz*™ *Bold & Bright*

cut 3

* This paper is also available by the sheet

Jack-in-the-Box

- patterned *Paper Pizazz*™: hearts and lines* (*Birthday*); purple with dots* (*Child's Play*)
- solid *Paper Pizazz*™: yellow, aqua, bright pink (*Plain Brights*)
- black pen: Zig

♥ Mat the body, arms, handle and heart as shown.

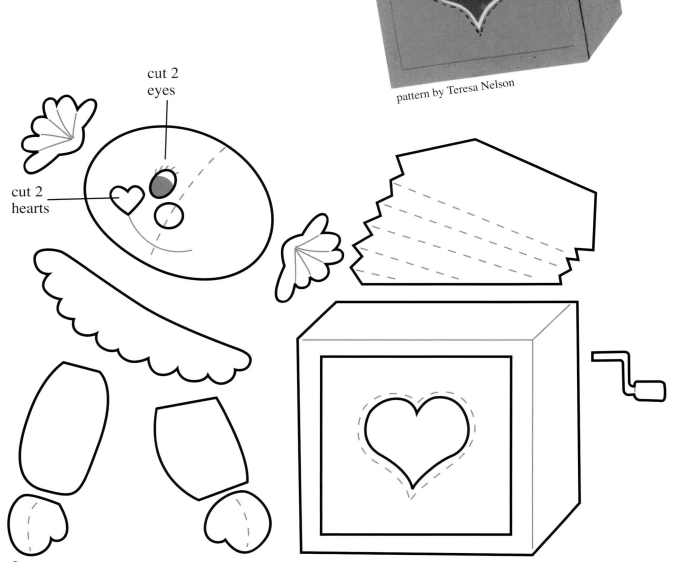

pattern by Teresa Nelson

cut 2 eyes

cut 2 hearts

* This paper is also available by the sheet

Juke Box

- patterned *Paper Pizazz*™: black with white dots* (*For Black & White Photos*); tie dye* (*Teen Years*); black with colored dots* (*Bright Great Backgrounds*); brown crushed suede* (*Black & White Photos*); black with colorful stripes (*Bold & Bright*)
- solid *Paper Pizazz*™: black, purple (*Solid Jewel Tones*); light brown (*Solid Muted Colors*)
- black pen: Marvy® Uchida

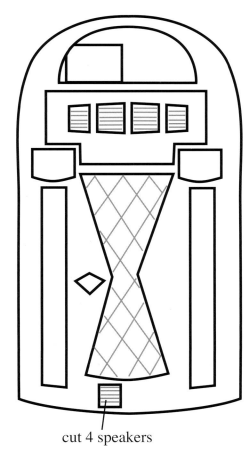

cut 4 speakers

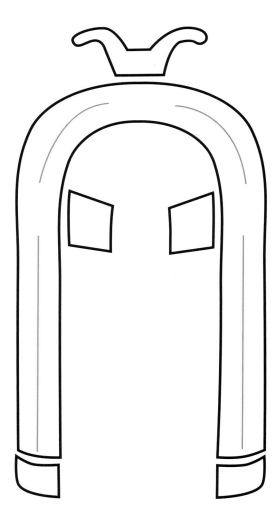

* This paper is also available by the sheet

Ladybug

- patterned *Paper Pizazz*™: red and black checks* (*Bold & Bright*); black with white dots* (*Coordinating Colors*™ *Orange & Black*)
- solid *Paper Pizazz*™: black (*Solid Jewel Tones*)
- black pen: Zig

Child in Ladybug Costume

- patterned *Paper Pizazz*™: yellow checks (*Bright Tints*); forest green suede*, black satin* (*Heritage Papers*); red and black check* (*Bold & Bright*)
- solid *Paper Pizazz*™: tan, white (*Plain Pastels*)
- pink decorating chalk: Craf-T Products
- cotton swab
- black pen: Zig
- white pen: Pentel

♥ Mat cape pieces on white.

pattern by Annie Lang

* This paper is also available by the sheet

Lamb

- patterned *Paper Pizazz*™: white moiré* (*Wedding*); blue dot (*Soft Tints*)
- solid *Paper Pizazz*™: mauve (*Solid Muted Colors*); black (*Solid Jewel Tones*)
- black pen: Zig
- white pen: Pentel

♥ Mat each piece on black.

quilt* paper from *Paper Pizazz*™ *Baby*

Jumping Lamb

- patterned *Paper Pizazz*™: vellum swirl* (*Vellum Papers*)
- solid *Paper Pizazz*™: white, light blue (*Plain Pastels*); black (*Solid Jewel Tones*)
- pink decorating chalk: Craf-T Products
- cotton swab
- black pen: Zig

♥ Mat legs on black.

cut 2 ears

Glue swirl vellum to light blue, then cut body and ears.

cut 4 hooves

Autumn Leaves

- patterned *Paper Pizazz*™: yellow check (*Bright Tints*); orange with white dots (*Coordinating Colors*™ *Orange & Black*); red with white dots* (*Christmas*)
- ¼" hole punch: McGill, Inc.
- black pen: Zig

plaid paper from *Coordinating Colors*™ *Orange & Black*; barnwood* paper from *Paper Pizazz*™ *Country*

patterns by Lisa Williams

* This paper is also available by the sheet

Leprechaun

- patterned *Paper Pizazz*™: green with tri-dots, green and white check (*Coordinating Colors*™ *Green & White*)
- solid *Paper Pizazz*™: dark green (*Coordinating Colors*™ *Green & White*); red, orange, green, yellow (*Plain Brights*); tan (*Plain Pastels*)
- black pen: Zig
- white pen: Pentel

pattern by Nance Wilhite-Kueneman

Menorah

- patterned *Paper Pizazz*™: brown velvet (*"Velvet" Backgrounds*); ivory crackled (*Textured Papers*); brown swirl* (*Black & White Photos*)
- solid *Paper Pizazz*™: black (*Solid Jewel Tones*)
- black pen: Zig

♥ Mat candles and menorah pieces on black.

cut 9 flames and 9 candles

Mittens

- patterned *Paper Pizazz*™: yellow diamonds (*Bright Tints*); green with white dots* (*Christmas*); red with white dots* (*Ho, Ho, Ho!!!*)
- solid *Paper Pizazz*™: white (*Plain Pastels*)
- black pen: Zig

♥ Mat each piece on white.

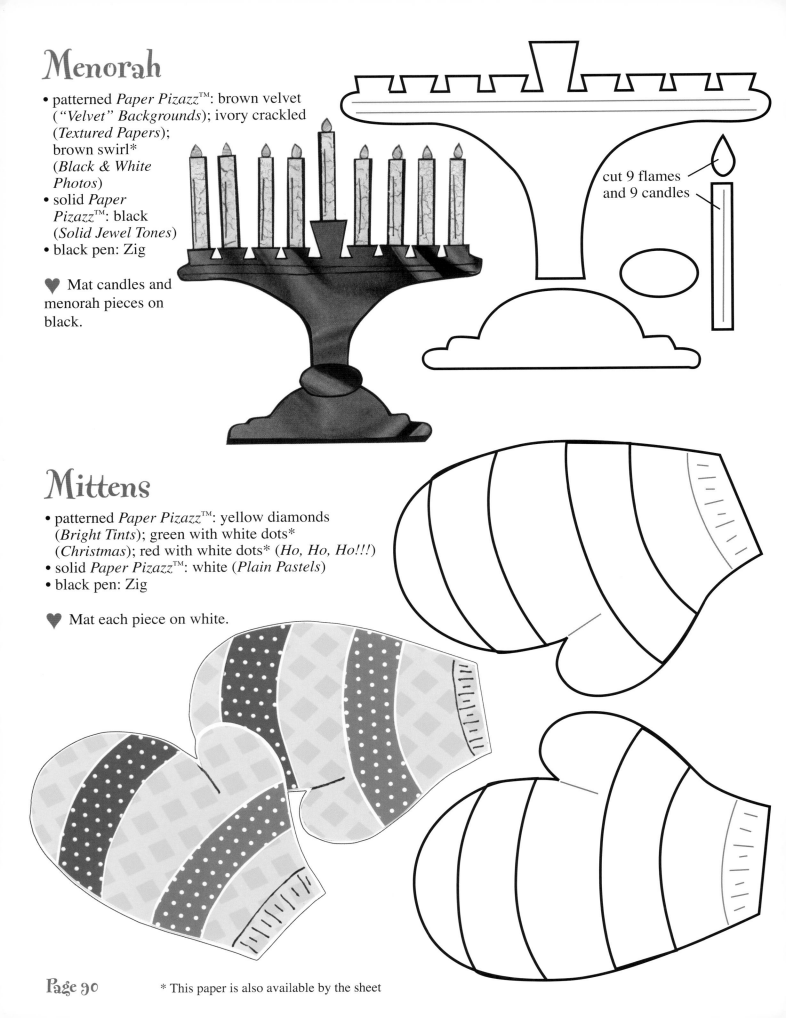

* This paper is also available by the sheet

Moon & Stars

- patterned *Paper Pizazz*™: blue textured (*Bright Great Backgrounds*); yellow checked (*Bright Tints*)
- solid *Paper Pizazz*™: dark pink, lavender (*Plain Pastels*)
- black pen: Zig
- pink pen: Pentel

pattern by Ruth Ninneman

Mortarboard

- patterned *Paper Pizazz*™: black satin* (*Heritage Papers*)
- solid *Paper Pizazz*™: white (*Plain Pastels*); red (*Plain Brights*); black (*Solid Jewel Tones*)
- black pen: Zig
- white pen: Pentel

♥ Mat pieces as shown.

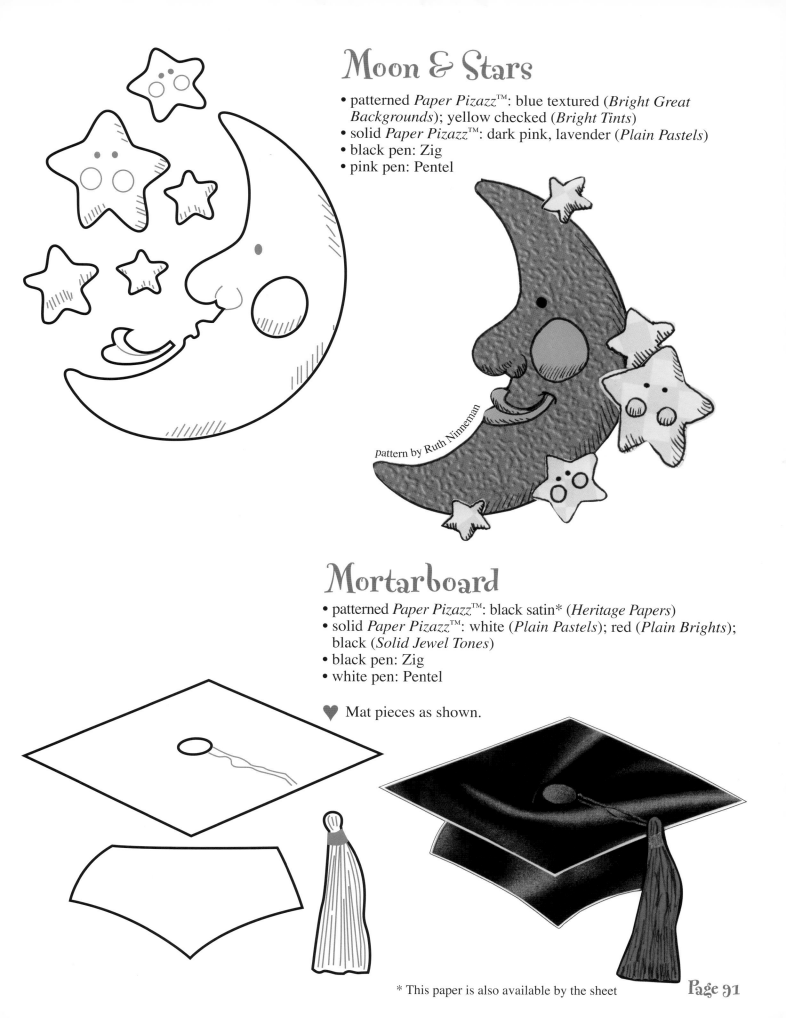

Motorcycle

- patterned *Paper Pizazz*™: black pinstripe, white with black stars, black with white dots*, black and white checks* (*Coordinating Colors*™ *Black & White*)
- solid *Paper Pizazz*™: specialty silver* (*Heavy Metals Papers*); specialty gold* (*Metallic Papers*); white (*Plain Pastels*)
- black pen: Zig

leather paper from *Paper Pizazz*™ *Textured Papers*

* This paper is also available by the sheet

Nativity Scene

- patterned *Paper Pizazz*™: purple satin* (*Bright Great Backgrounds*); barnwood* (*Country*); grass* (*Pets*); white moiré* (*Wedding*); gold sponged stars* (*Spattered, Crackled, Sponged*); forest green suede* (*Making Heritage Scrapbook Pages*); navy suede* (*Heritage Papers*)
- solid *Paper Pizazz*™: peach, brown (*Solid Muted Colors*)
- black and brown pens: Zig
- gold pen (*Pentel*)

Noah's Ark

- patterned *Paper Pizazz*™: barnwood* (*Country*); elephant skin (*Wild Things*); yellow stripes (*Soft Tints*)
- solid *Paper Pizazz*™: dark brown, black (*Solid Jewel Tones*); pink (*Plain Pastels*)
- scallop and deckle scissors: Fiskars
- red decorating chalk: Craf-T Products
- cotton swab
- black pen: Zig

♥ Mat ark, roof and house pieces on black.

animal patterns by Ruth Ninneman

cut 2 of each giraffe piece

cut 2

cut 2

cut 8-10

cut 8-10

Roof: Trim three 1" wide brown strips with scallop scissors. Glue overlapped and cut roof shapes.

Ark: Glue the wood shingles to the ark as shown, allowing the ends to extend beyond the ark. Let dry, then trim the shingles even with the ark.

Paintbrush

- patterned *Paper Pizazz*™: brown corrugated*, barnwood* (*Country*); specialty silver* (*Heavy Metals Papers*)
- solid *Paper Pizazz*™: black (*Solid Jewel Tones*)
- mini-pinking scissors: Fiskars
- black pen: Zig

♥ Mat each piece on black.

← 1½ →

↑ 1½ ↓

* This paper is also available by the sheet

Palm Tree

- patterned *Paper Pizazz*™: sand (*Textured Papers*); brown crushed suede* (*Black & White Photos*); grass* (*Pets*)
- black pen: Zig

Party Hat

- patterned *Paper Pizazz*™: purple with dots* (*Child's Play*)
- solid *Paper Pizazz*™: red, blue (*Plain Brights*)
- black pen: Zig

♥ Mat stripes on black.

* This paper is also available by the sheet

Pencil

- patterned *Paper Pizazz*™: yellow squiggle (*Soft Tints*)
- solid *Paper Pizazz*™: gray, black (*Solid Jewel Tones*); tan, pink (*Plain Pastels*)
- black pen: Zig
- white pen: Pentel

♥ Mat each piece on black.

Penguin

- patterned *Paper Pizazz*™: black and white plaid* (*For Black & White Photos*); black with white dots* (*Heritage Papers*)
- solid *Paper Pizazz*™: black (*Solid Jewel Tones*); white, golden yellow, blue (*Plain Pastels*); vellum (*Vellum Papers*)
- pink decorating chalk: Craf-T Products
- cotton swab
- black pen: Zig

♥ Mat each piece on black or white as shown.

pattern by Annie Lang

Cut 1 ice cube from vellum and 1 from blue. Glue the vellum cube between the arms and the blue cube behind the left arm.

* This paper is also available by the sheet

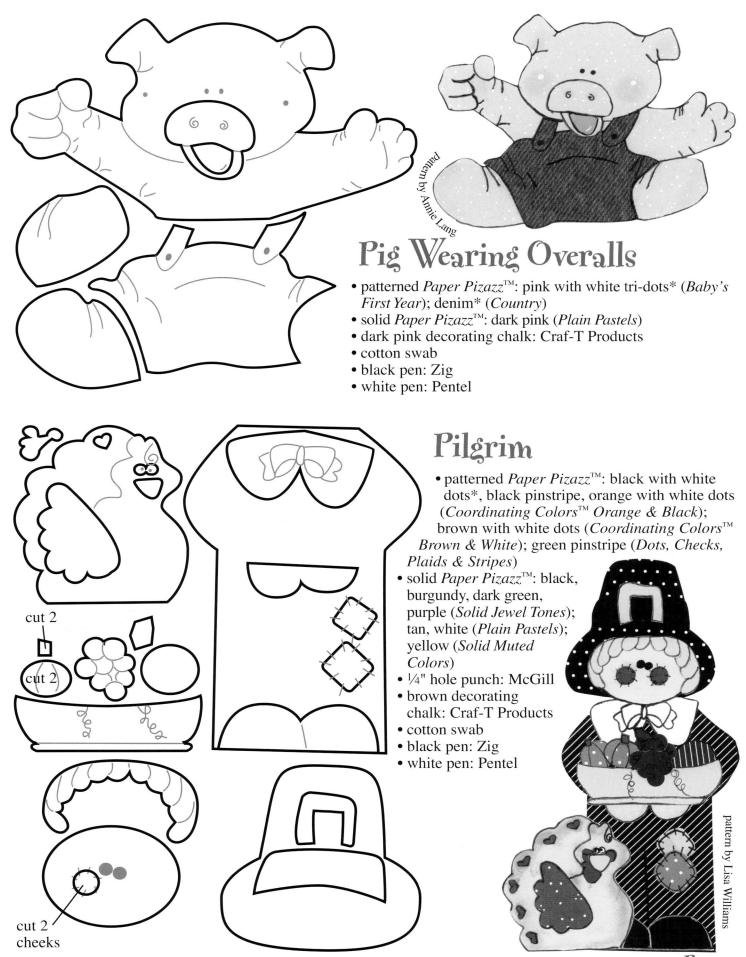

Pig Wearing Overalls

- patterned *Paper Pizazz*™: pink with white tri-dots* (*Baby's First Year*); denim* (*Country*)
- solid *Paper Pizazz*™: dark pink (*Plain Pastels*)
- dark pink decorating chalk: Craf-T Products
- cotton swab
- black pen: Zig
- white pen: Pentel

Pilgrim

- patterned *Paper Pizazz*™: black with white dots*, black pinstripe, orange with white dots (*Coordinating Colors*™ *Orange & Black*); brown with white dots (*Coordinating Colors*™ *Brown & White*); green pinstripe (*Dots, Checks, Plaids & Stripes*)
- solid *Paper Pizazz*™: black, burgundy, dark green, purple (*Solid Jewel Tones*); tan, white (*Plain Pastels*); yellow (*Solid Muted Colors*)
- ¼" hole punch: McGill
- brown decorating chalk: Craf-T Products
- cotton swab
- black pen: Zig
- white pen: Pentel

cut 2

cut 2

cut 2
cheeks

* This paper is also available by the sheet

Poinsettia

- patterned *Paper Pizazz*™: burgundy velvet, blue velvet, green velvet (*"Velvet" Backgrounds*)
- solid *Paper Pizazz*™: specialty gold* (*Metallic Papers*); ivory (*Plain Pastels*)
- ⅜" hole punch: McGill, Inc.
- black pen: Zig

cut 8 for flower centers

cut 5 berries

* This paper is also available by the sheet

Popcorn

cut 15-20 pieces of popcorn

- patterned *Paper Pizazz*™: red and white stripe* (*Ho, Ho, Ho!!!*)
- solid *Paper Pizazz*™: black (*Solid Jewel Tones*); yellow (*Plain Brights*); white (*Plain Pastels*)
- black pen: Zig

♥ Mat each piece on yellow or black as shown.

For a great look, cut the entire popcorn shape from the popcorn paper in *Paper Pizazz*™ *Yummy Papers*.

Popsicle

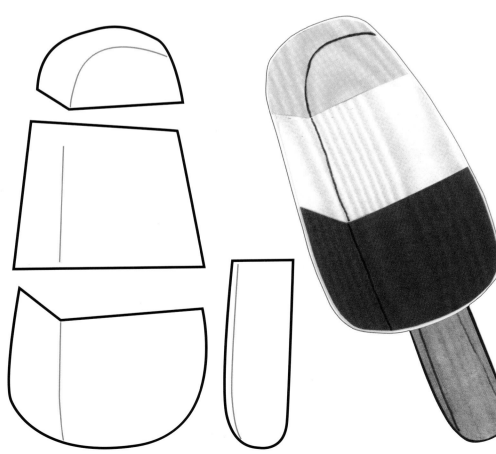

- patterned *Paper Pizazz*™: pink moiré*, white moiré* (*Wedding*); purple moiré* (*Pretty Papers*); barnwood* (*Country*)
- solid *Paper Pizazz*™: white (*Plain Pastels*); black (*Solid Jewel Tones*)
- black pen: Zig

♥ Mat the pieces on black or white as shown.

* This paper is also available by the sheet

Happy Birthday Present

- patterned *Paper Pizazz*™: pink swirl, yellow dots (*Soft Tints*)
- solid *Paper Pizazz*™: white, dark pink (*Plain Pastels*)
- X-acto® knife
- cutting surface
- black pen: Zig

Change the papers to make this present fit your needs—Christmas, a baby shower, wedding, etc.

ribbon

ribbon

Pumpkin

- patterned *Paper Pizazz*™: green with white dots* (*Christmas*); orange with white dots (*Coordinating Colors*™ *Orange & Black*); yellow check (*Bright Tints*)
- solid *Paper Pizazz*™: brown (*Solid Jewel Tones*); yellow, red (*Plain Brights*)
- black pen: Zig

pattern by Lisa Williams

Glue vellum swirl to pink, then trace and cut the top of the rattle.

Baby Rattle

- patterned *Paper Pizazz*™: green swirl, blue dots (*Soft Tints*); vellum swirl* (*Vellum Papers*)
- solid *Paper Pizazz*™: pink (*Plain Pastels*)
- black pen: Zig

* This paper is also available by the sheet

Rocking Horse

- patterned *Paper Pizazz*™: pink and yellow plaid*; green, yellow and pink plaid* (*Pastel Plaids*)
- solid *Paper Pizazz*™: pink, pale yellow (*Plain Pastels*)
- black pen: Zig

♥ Mat pieces on yellow as shown.
★ Mat the finished piece on yellow.

pattern by Teresa Nelson

cut 2

* This paper is also available by the sheet

Long-Stemmed Rose

- patterned *Paper Pizazz*™: forest green suede* (*Making Heritage Scrapbook Pages*); burgundy suede* (*Heritage Papers*)
- solid *Paper Pizazz*™: black (*Solid Jewel Tones*)
- black pen: Zig

♥ Mat each piece on black.

#1

The rose and rosebud are assembled in layers for a three-dimensional look. The numbers give the order of the layers, starting with #1 on the bottom. The red lines guide you in placing the next layer. The patterns on this page are for the rose; the bud, stem and leaf patterns are on page 104.

#2

#3

#4

#5

#6

#7

#8

#9

Long-Stemmed Rose (cont'd)

#1

#2

#3

#4

#5

There are numerous variations you can use with this rose pattern. Make a yellow rose for friendship or a pink one for romance, varying the color used to mat the petals. Or piece just the flower or bud on separate stems, each with a few leaves.

laser lace* from *Paper Pizazz*™ *Romantic Papers*; red velvet paper from *Paper Pizazz*™ *"Velvet" Backgrounds*

* This paper is also available by the sheet

RV

- patterned *Paper Pizazz*™: white moiré* (*Wedding*); denim* (*Country*); red with tri-dots* (*Dots, Checks, Plaids & Stripes*); vellum swirl* (*Vellum Papers*)
- solid *Paper Pizazz*™: black (*Solid Jewel Tones*); yellow (*Plain Brights*)

Cut out the windows with scissors or an X-acto® knife, then line the edges with black. Cut a large piece of vellum swirl and glue it behind the design.

♥ Mat each piece except tires and windows on black.

map paper from *Paper Pizazz*™ *Our Vacation*; road sign Punch-Outs™ from *Paper Pizazz*™ *Our Vacation Punch-Outs*™

* This paper is also available by the sheet

Sail Boat

- patterned *Paper Pizazz*™: blue swirl (*Light Great Backgrounds*); blue paisley (*Bright Great Backgrounds*); barnwood* (*Country*)
- solid *Paper Pizazz*™: black (*Solid Jewel Tones*); white (*Plain Pastels*)
- 5⁄8" star punch: Marvy® Uchida
- black pen: Zig

Sand Bucket & Shovel

- patterned *Paper Pizazz*™: red with white dots* (*Bright Great Backgrounds*)
- solid *Paper Pizazz*™: red, yellow, aqua (*Plain Brights*)
- black pen: Zig

cut 5

* This paper is also available by the sheet

Sand Castle

- patterned *Paper Pizazz*™: sand (*Textured Papers*)
- solid *Paper Pizazz*™: black (*Solid Jewel Tones*)
- black pen: Zig

♥ Mat each piece on black.

pattern by Ruth Ninneman

cut 3

cut 3

Celestial Santa

- patterned *Paper Pizazz*™: gold sponged stars* (*A Woman's Scrapbook*); red and white stripe (*Stripes, Checks & Dots*)
- solid *Paper Pizazz*™: black, red (*Solid Jewel Tones*); white (*Plain Pastels*)
- black pen: Zig
- pink colored pencil: Prang

♥ Mat each piece on black.

pattern by Nance Wilhite-Kueneman

cut 2 hands

* This paper is also available by the sheet

Chimney Santa

- patterned *Paper Pizazz*™: brick wall (*Masculine Papers*); burlap* (*Country*); burgundy suede* (*Heritage Papers*); vellum snowflakes* (*Vellum Papers*)
- solid *Paper Pizazz*™: black (*Solid Jewel Tones*); specialty gold* (*Metallic Papers*); cream, pink (*Plain Pastels*)
- pink decorating chalk: Craf-T Products
- cotton swab
- black pen: Zig
- white pen: Pentel

cut 3

cut 3

cut 2

Ho Ho Ho Santa

- patterned *Paper Pizazz*™: snowflakes*, red with white dots* (*Ho, Ho, Ho!!!*); green with white dots* (*Christmas*)
- solid *Paper Pizazz*™: white, dark pink, tan (*Plain Pastels*); red, green (*Plain Brights*); black (*Solid Jewel Tones*)
- ¼" hole punch: McGill, Inc.
- ⅝" spiral punch: Family Treasures
- deckle scissors: Fiskars
- pink decorating chalk: Craf-T Products
- cotton swab
- X-acto® knife
- cutting surface
- black pen: Zig

♥ Mat letters on black.

The patterns for Santa's face and beard are on page 111.

cut 2

cut 2

cut 3

* This paper is also available by the sheet

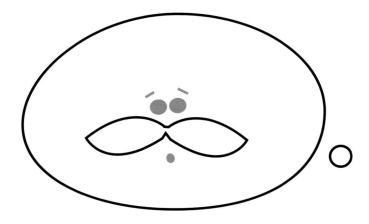

cut 9

Rustic Santa

- patterned *Paper Pizazz*™: ivory crackled (*Textured Papers*); red with white tri-dots*, forest green pinstripe* (*Dots, Checks, Plaids & Stripes*)
- solid *Paper Pizazz*™: ivory, tan (*Plain Pastels*); yellow, blue (*Solid Muted Colors*)
- ½" star punch: Family Treasures
- brown and pink decorating chalk: Craf-T Products
- cotton swab
- black pen: Zig
- white pen: Pentel

pattern by Temple Garman

Waving Santa

- patterned *Paper Pizazz*™: ivory crackled, burgundy velvet, teal brocade, white lace (*Textured Papers*); black satin (*Heritage Papers*)
- solid *Paper Pizazz*™: specialty gold* (*Metallic Papers*); tan (*Plain Pastels*); mauve (*Solid Muted Colors*)
- pink decorating chalk: Craf-T Products
- cotton swab
- black pen: Zig

cut 2

cut 2 buttons

cut 2

* This paper is also available by the sheet

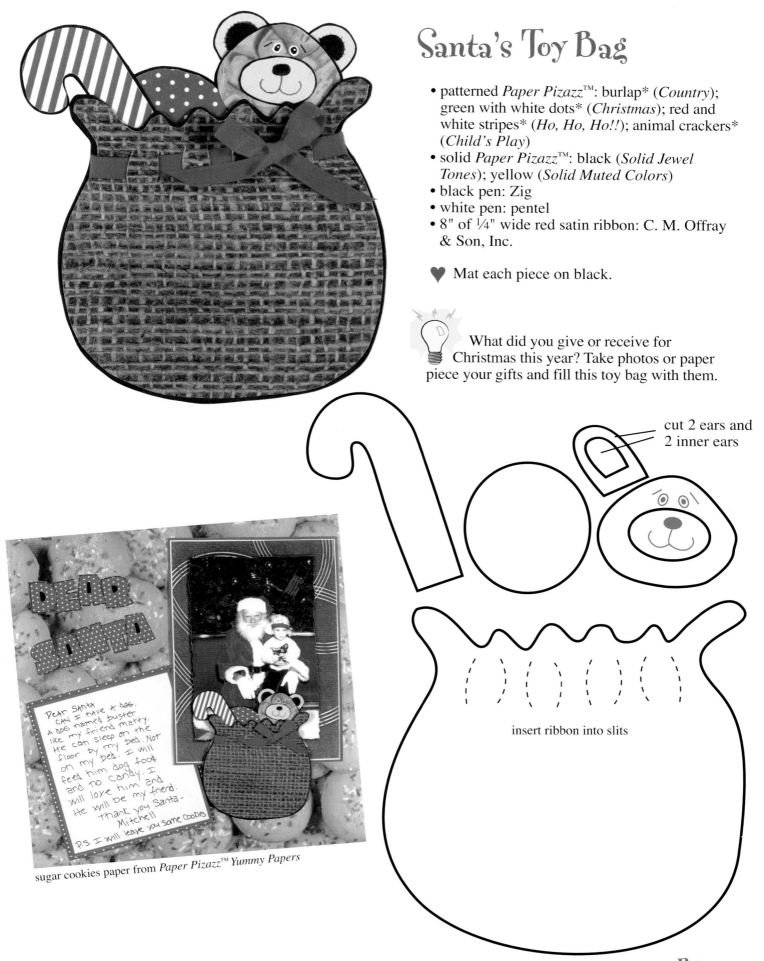

Santa's Toy Bag

- patterned *Paper Pizazz*™: burlap* (*Country*); green with white dots* (*Christmas*); red and white stripes* (*Ho, Ho, Ho!!*); animal crackers* (*Child's Play*)
- solid *Paper Pizazz*™: black (*Solid Jewel Tones*); yellow (*Solid Muted Colors*)
- black pen: Zig
- white pen: pentel
- 8" of ¼" wide red satin ribbon: C. M. Offray & Son, Inc.

♥ Mat each piece on black.

What did you give or receive for Christmas this year? Take photos or paper piece your gifts and fill this toy bag with them.

cut 2 ears and 2 inner ears

insert ribbon into slits

sugar cookies paper from *Paper Pizazz*™ *Yummy Papers*

Dear Santa
Can I have a dog.
A dog named buster
like my friend matty.
He can sleep on the
floor by my bed. Not
on my bed. I will
feed him dog food
and no candy. I
will love him and
He will be my friend.
Thank you Santa-
Mitchell
P.S. I will leave you some cookies

Scarecrow

- patterned *Paper Pizazz*™: gold, brown and rust plaid* (*Jewel Plaids*); denim*, burlap* (*Country*); orange with white dots (*Coordinating Colors*™ *Orange & Black*)
- solid *Paper Pizazz*™: ivory, yellow (*Plain Pastels*); orange, green (*Plain Brights*); brown, black (*Solid Jewel Tones*)
- pink decorating chalk: Craf-T Products
- cotton swab
- 8" of single-ply jute twine
- paper corrugator
- black pen: Zig

The patterns for the pumpkin, scarecrow's head and hat are on page 115.

Run paper through a paper corrugator, then cut from it 20-30 strands of hay.

pattern by Nance Wilhite-Kueneman

* This paper is also available by the sheet

Scarecrow (cont'd)

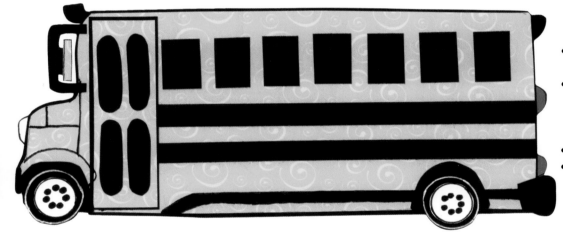

School Bus

- patterned *Paper Pizazz*™: yellow swirl (*Bright Tints*)
- solid *Paper Pizazz*™: black (*Solid Jewel Tones*); white (*Plain Pastels*); red (*Plain Brights*)
- black pen: Zig
- white pen: Pentel

♥ Mat bus and door on black.

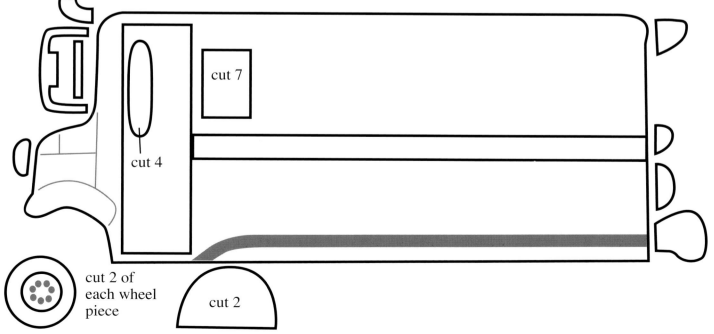

cut 7

cut 4

cut 2 of each wheel piece

cut 2

School House

- patterned *Paper Pizazz*™: brick (*Textured Papers*); blue corrugated (*Country*)
- solid *Paper Pizazz*™: specialty gold* (*Metallic Papers*); black (*Solid Jewel Tones*); white (*Plain Pastels*)
- black pen: Zig

♥ Mat each piece on black as shown.

blackboard paper from *Paper Pizazz*™ *Our School Days*; crayons* paper from *Paper Pizazz*™ *School Days*

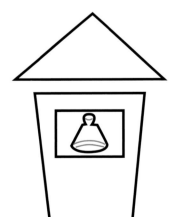

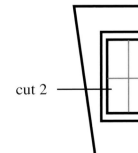

cut 2

* This paper is also available by the sheet

Scissors

- patterned *Paper Pizazz*™: red with tri-dots* (*Dots, Checks & Stripes*)
- solid *Paper Pizazz*™: yellow, blue (*Plain Brights*); black (*Solid Jewel Tones*)

♥ Mat each piece on black.

Seashell

- patterned *Paper Pizazz*™: pink with white dots (*Lisa Williams Pink, Lavender & Beige*)
- solid *Paper Pizazz*™: black (*Solid Jewel Tones*)

♥ Mat each piece on black.

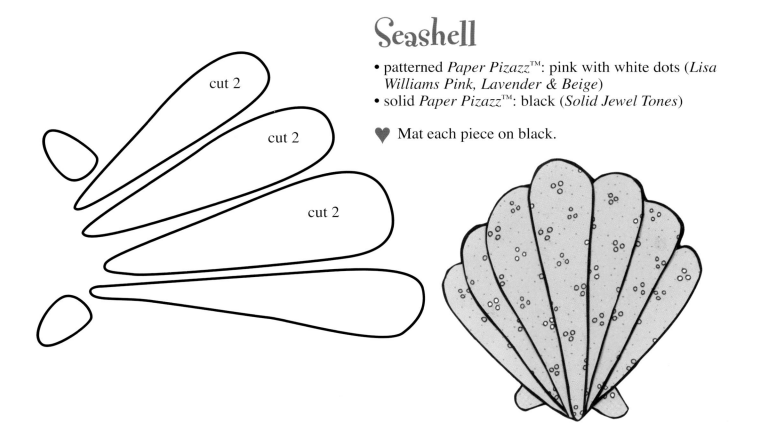

cut 2

cut 2

cut 2

Shirt & Tie

- patterned *Paper Pizazz*™: yellow dots (*Bright Tints*); yellow and blue plaid (*Jewel Plaids*)
- solid *Paper Pizazz*™: black (*Solid Jewel Tones*)
- black Pen: Zig

♥ Mat each piece on black.

Shoe, Baby

- patterned *Paper Pizazz*™: colorful dots* (*School Days*); brown sponged (*Spattered, Crackled, Sponged*)
- solid *Paper Pizazz*™: light blue (*Plain Pastels*)
- black pen: Zig

* This paper is also available by the sheet

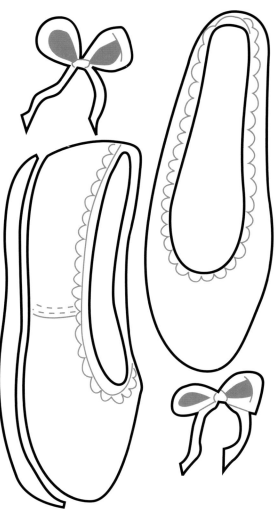

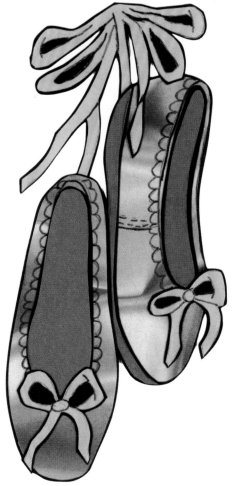

Shoes, Ballet

- patterned *Paper Pizazz*™: pink satin* (*Pretty Papers*); light blue moiré* (*Light Great Backgrounds*)
- solid *Paper Pizazz*™: black (*Solid Jewel Tones*); mauve (*Solid Muted Colors*)
- black pen: Zig

♥ Mat each piece on black.

Shoes, Girl's

cut 2 of every piece

- patterned *Paper Pizazz*™: black dots* (*Black & White Photos*); pink moiré*, white moiré* (*Wedding*)
- solid *Paper Pizazz*™: white (*Plain Pastels*); black (*Solid Jewel Tones*)
- ¼" hole punch: McGill
- black pen: Zig

♥ Mat pieces on black or white as shown.

* This paper is also available by the sheet

Page 119

Skateboard

- patterned *Paper Pizazz*™: geometric pattern (*Bright Great Backgrounds*)
- solid *Paper Pizazz*™: black (*Solid Jewel Tones*); aqua (*Plain Brights*); white (*Plain Pastels*)
- black pen: Zig

cut 2 wheels

cut 2 wheel centers

cut 2 wheels for the opposite side of the skateboard

Ski Cap

- patterned *Paper Pizazz*™: yellow diamonds (*Bright Tints*); red with white dots* (*Ho, Ho, Ho!!!*); green with white dots* (*Christmas*)
- solid *Paper Pizazz*™: white (*Plain Pastels*)
- black pen: Zig

♥ Mat each piece on white.

insert hat

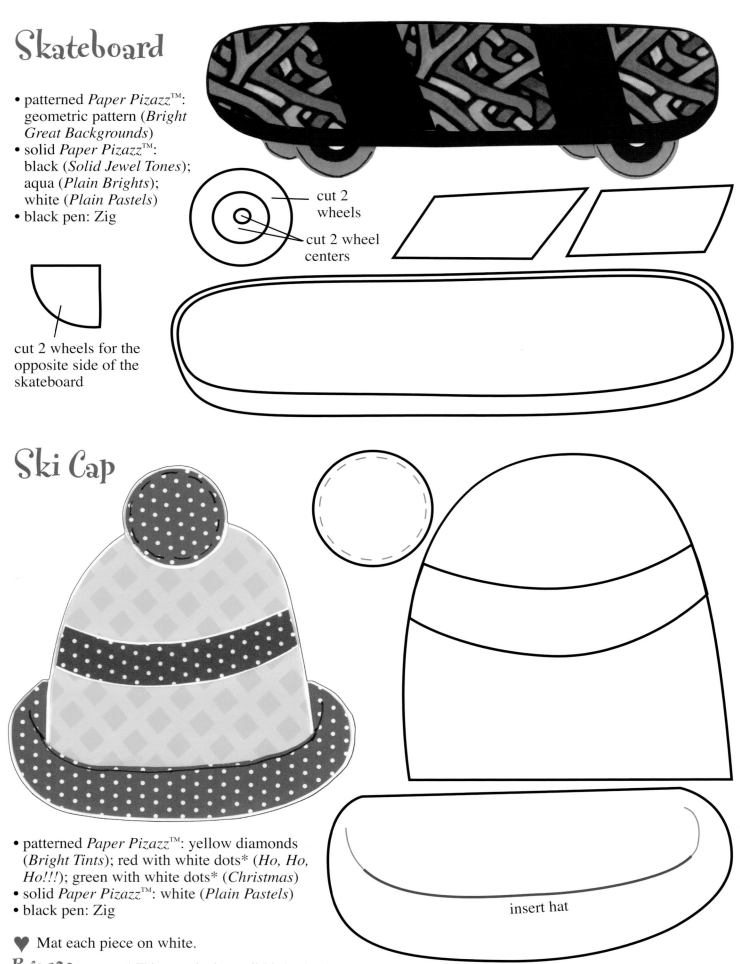

* This paper is also available by the sheet

Snowman with Star or Heart

- patterned *Paper Pizazz*™: burgundy with tri-dots*, green pinstripe* (*Dots, Checks, Plaids & Stripes*)
- solid *Paper Pizazz*™: mauve (*Solid Muted Colors*); white, tan (*Plain Pastels*)
- ⅛" hole, ⅝" circle, 1⅛" star punches: McGill, Inc.
- pink decorating chalk: Craf-T Products
- cotton swab
- green and black pens: Zig

The patterns for the star and heart are on page 122.

pattern by Nance Wilhite-Kueneman

LET IT SNOW

Snowman with Star or Heart (cont'd)

LET IT SNOW

Waving Snowman

- patterned *Paper Pizazz*™: ivory crackled (*Textured Papers*); red plaid (*Jewel Plaids*); red with white dots* (*Ho, Ho, Ho!!!*); green with white dots* (*Christmas*); orange with white dots (*Coordinating Colors*™ *Orange & Black*)
- solid *Paper Pizazz*™: tan (*Solid Muted Colors*); black (*Solid Jewel Tones*)
- black pen: Zig
- white pen: Pentel

♥ Mat each piece on black.

pattern by Diane Bliss

cut 2

cut 2

* This paper is also available by the sheet

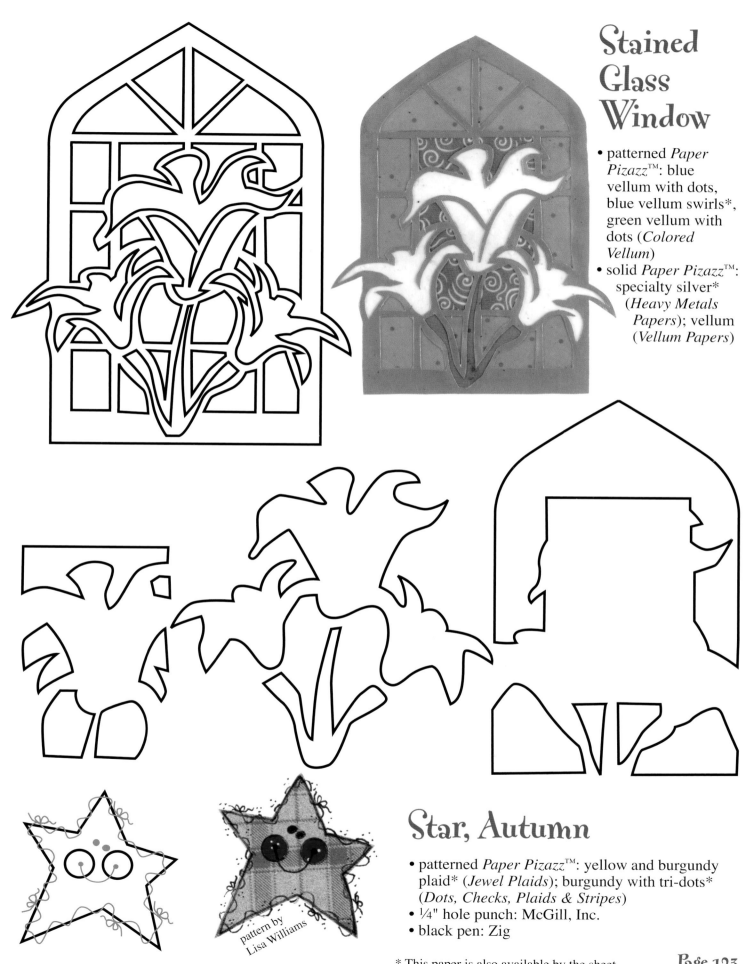

Stained Glass Window

- patterned *Paper Pizazz™*: blue vellum with dots, blue vellum swirls*, green vellum with dots (*Colored Vellum*)
- solid *Paper Pizazz™*: specialty silver* (*Heavy Metals Papers*); vellum (*Vellum Papers*)

Star, Autumn

pattern by Lisa Williams

- patterned *Paper Pizazz™*: yellow and burgundy plaid* (*Jewel Plaids*); burgundy with tri-dots* (*Dots, Checks, Plaids & Stripes*)
- ¼" hole punch: McGill, Inc.
- black pen: Zig

* This paper is also available by the sheet

Page 123

Stocking, Victorian

- patterned *Paper Pizazz*™: laser lace* (*Romantic Papers*); blue velvet, burgundy velvet, green velvet, purple velvet (*"Velvet" Backgrounds*)
- solid *Paper Pizazz*™: ivory (*Plain Pastels*)
- mini scallop and scallop scissors: Fiskars
- ½" circle punch: Marvy® Uchida
- black pen: Zig

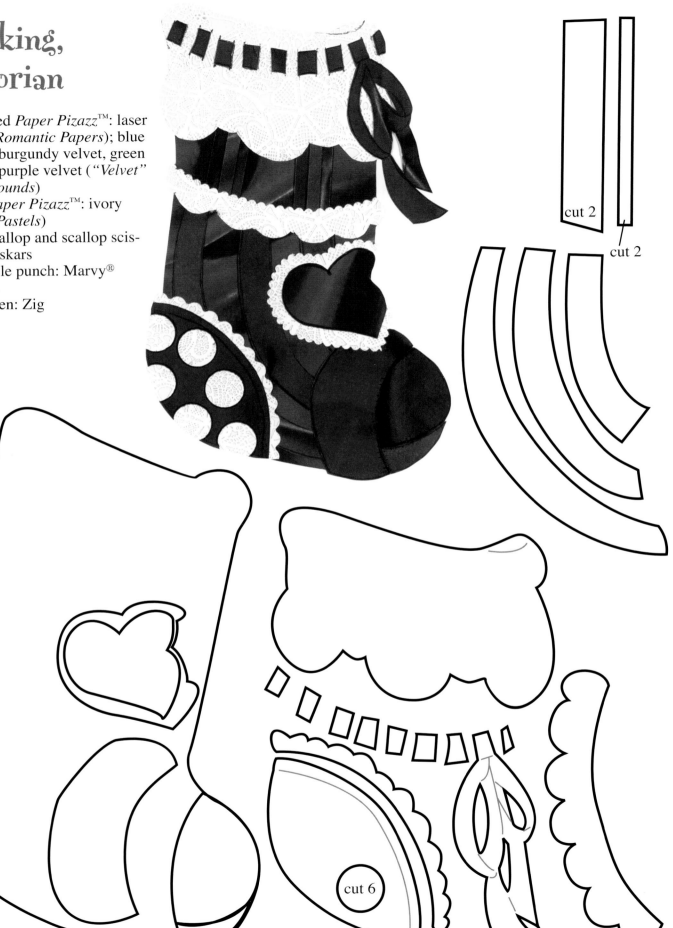

cut 2

cut 2

cut 6

* This paper is also available by the sheet

Strawberries

- patterned *Paper Pizazz*™: red with tri-dots* (*Dots, Checks, Plaids & Stripes*); green velvet (*"Velvet" Backgrounds*)
- solid *Paper Pizazz*™: white (*Plain Pastels*)
- black pen: Zig
- yellow pen: Pentel

Pattern by Ruth Ninneman

strawberry paper from *Paper Pizazz*™ *Yummy Papers*; vellum with dots* from *Paper Pizazz*™ *Vellum Papers*

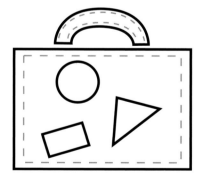

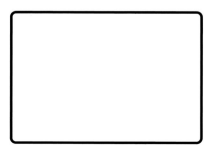

Suitcase

- patterned *Paper Pizazz*™: colorful dots* (*Bright Great Backgrounds*); yellow check, green check, blue check (*Bright Tints*)
- solid *Paper Pizazz*™: black (*Solid Jewel Tones*)
- black pen: Zig

♥ Mat each piece on black.

Smiling Sun

- patterned *Paper Pizazz*™: yellow checks, yellow swirl (*Bright Tints*); colorful argyle (*Bold & Bright*)
- solid *Paper Pizazz*™: black (*Solid Jewel Tones*); pink, white (*Plain Pastels*)
- black pen: Zig

♥ Mat plaid and check circles on black.

pattern by Ruth Ninneman

cut 2

Sunglasses

- patterned *Paper Pizazz*™: black satin* (*Heritage Papers*); green with white dots* (*Christmas*)
- black pen: Zig

* This paper is also available by the sheet

Tea Cup & Teapot

- patterned *Paper Pizazz*™: pink and yellow check, pink flower, yellow wave (*Soft Tints*)
- solid *Paper Pizazz*™: white, yellow (*Solid Pastels*)
- ½" wide circle punch: Marvy® Uchida
- ¼" hole, 1" heart punch: McGill, Inc.
- ½" flower punch: Family Treasures
- black pen: Zig

patterns by Nance Wilhite-Kueneman

yellow diamonds paper from *Paper Pizazz*™ *Soft Tints*

Tee-Shirt

- patterned *Paper Pizazz*™: tie dye* (*Teen Years*)
- solid *Paper Pizazz*™: black (*Solid Jewel Tones*)
- black pen: Zig

★ Mat the finished piece on black.

Tent

- patterned *Paper Pizazz*™: brown plaid* (*Great Outdoors*); brown crushed suede* (*Black & White Photos*); brown velvet (*"Velvet" Backgrounds*)
- solid *Paper Pizazz*™: gray (*Solid Jewel Tones*)
- black pen: Zig

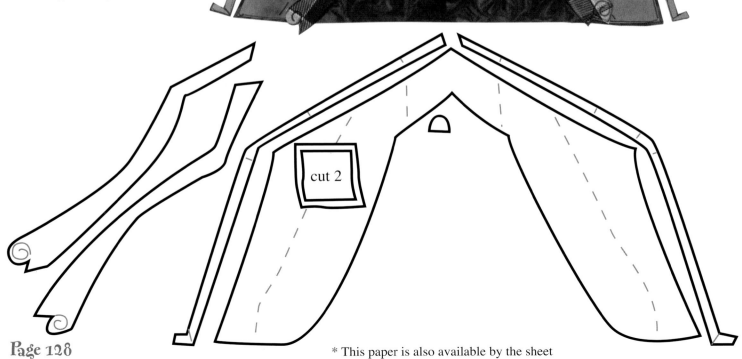

* This paper is also available by the sheet

Tools: Hammer

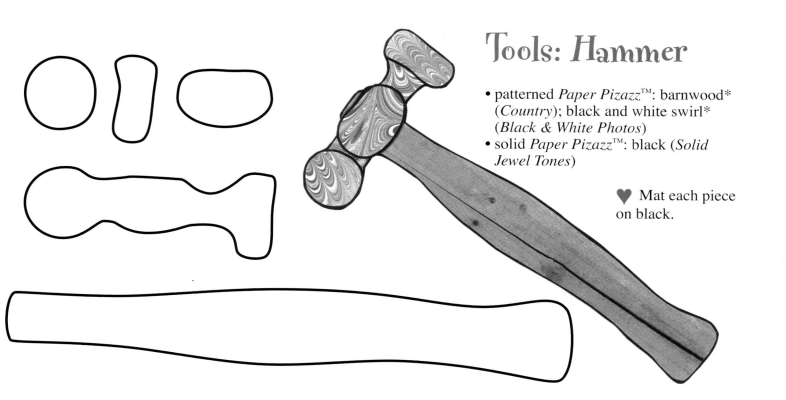

- patterned *Paper Pizazz*™: barnwood* (*Country*); black and white swirl* (*Black & White Photos*)
- solid *Paper Pizazz*™: black (*Solid Jewel Tones*)

♥ Mat each piece on black.

Tools: Pipe Wrench

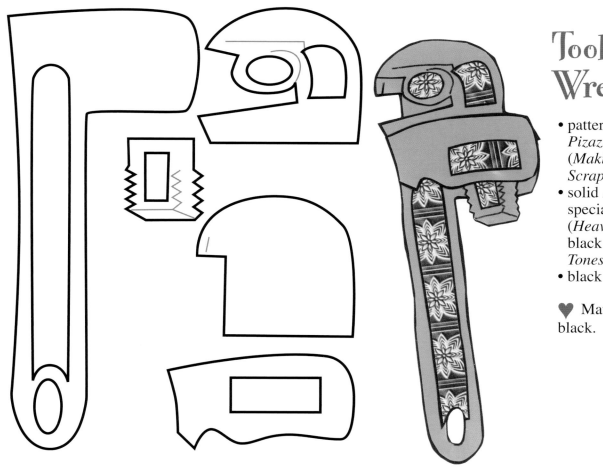

- patterned *Paper Pizazz*™: silver tiles (*Making Heritage Scrapbook Pages*)
- solid *Paper Pizazz*™: specialty silver* (*Heavy Metals Papers*); black (*Solid Jewel Tones*)
- black pen: Zig

♥ Mat each piece on black.

* This paper is also available by the sheet

Tools: Pliers

- patterned *Paper Pizazz*™: screenwork (*Textured Papers*)
- solid *Paper Pizazz*™: black (*Solid Jewel Tones*)
- black pen: Zig

♥ Mat each piece on black.

Tools: Saw

- patterned *Paper Pizazz*™: barnwood* (*Country*)
- solid *Paper Pizazz*™: specialty silver* (*Heavy Metals Papers*)
- mini pinking scissors: Fiskars

♥ Mat each piece on black.

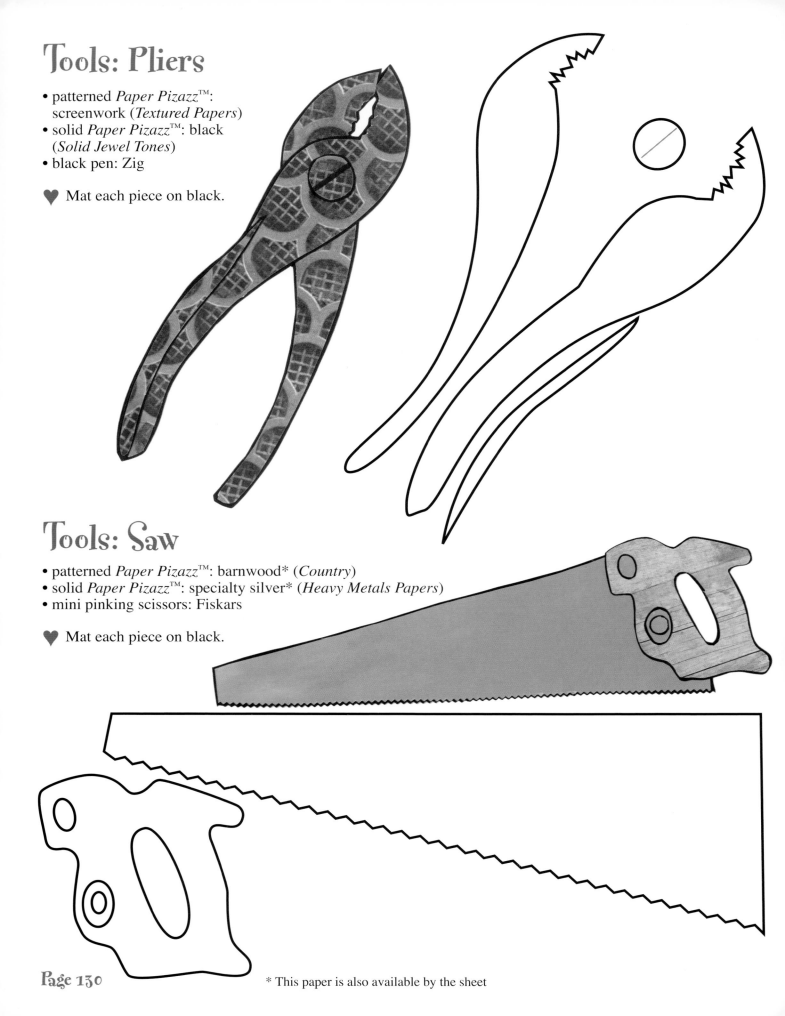

* This paper is also available by the sheet

Tools: Screwdriver

- patterned *Paper Pizazz™*: red with hollow dots* (*Bold & Bright*)
- solid *Paper Pizazz™*: specialty silver* (*Heavy Metals Papers*); black (*Solid Jewel Tones*)
- black pen: Zig

♥ Mat each piece on black.

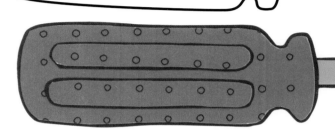

cut 2

Top Hat

- patterned *Paper Pizazz™*: black with dots* (*Black & White photos*); black satin* (*Heritage Papers*)
- solid *Paper Pizazz™*: white (*Plain Pastels*)
- white pen: Pentel

♥ Mat each piece on white.

* This paper is also available by the sheet

Toy Soldiers

- patterned *Paper Pizazz*™: black satin* , navy suede* (*Heritage Papers*); red moiré* (*Black & White Photos*); gold sponged stars* (*Spattered, Crackled, Sponged*)
- solid *Paper Pizazz*™: specialty gold* (*Metallic Papers*); black (*Solid Jewel Tones*); pale yellow (*Plain Pastels*)
- black and red pens: Zig
- white pen: Pentel
- gold pen: Zebra

♥ Mat each piece on black.

cut 2 cheeks

* This paper is also available by the sheet

Train

- patterned *Paper Pizazz*™: yellow check (*Bright Tints*); purple with dots* (*Childhood*); colorful stripes* (*Birthday*); red with dots* (*Bright Great Backgrounds*)
- solid *Paper Pizazz*™: black (*Solid Jewel Tones*); yellow, green, aqua, red (*Plain Brights*); white (*Plain Pastels*)

♥ Mat each piece on black.

cut 2

cut 3

cut 3

cut 6

cut 6

Trophy

- patterned *Paper Pizazz*™: brown swirl* (*Black & White Photos*); gold sponged stars* (*Spattered, Crackled, Sponged*)
- black pen: Zig

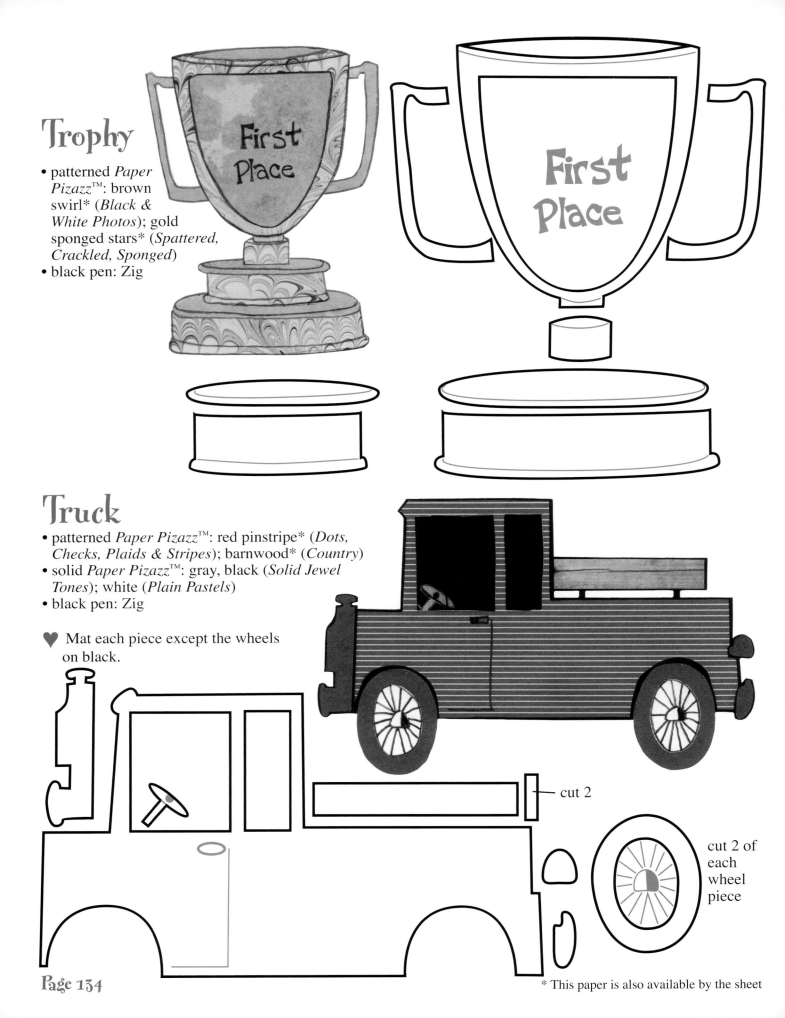

Truck

- patterned *Paper Pizazz*™: red pinstripe* (*Dots, Checks, Plaids & Stripes*); barnwood* (*Country*)
- solid *Paper Pizazz*™: gray, black (*Solid Jewel Tones*); white (*Plain Pastels*)
- black pen: Zig

♥ Mat each piece except the wheels on black.

cut 2

cut 2 of each wheel piece

* This paper is also available by the sheet

Child in Turkey Costume

pattern by Annie Lang

- patterned *Paper Pizazz*™: brown plaid (*Coordinating Colors*™ *Flannel Plaids*); brown with hollow dots (*Coordinating Colors*™ *Brown & White*); yellow check, yellow and red plaid (*Bright Tints*)
- solid *Paper Pizazz*™: black, brown (*Solid Jewel Tones*); tan (*Plain Pastels*)
- pink decorating chalk: Craf-T Products
- cotton swab
- black pen: Zig

♥ Mat each piece on black.

cut 6

* This paper is also available by the sheet   **Page 135**

Thanksgiving Turkey

- patterned *Paper Pizazz*™: burgundy with tri-dots*, dark green pinstripe* (*Dots, Checks, Stripes & Plaids*); brown with white stars (*Coordinating Colors*™ *Brown & White*); orange plaid (*Coordinating Colors*™ *Orange & Black*)
- solid *Paper Pizazz*™: black, brown, burgundy (*Solid Jewel Tones*); peach (*Solid Muted Colors*); tan (*Plain Pastels*)
- black pen: Zig

★ Mat the finished piece on black.

pattern by Nance Wilhite-Kueneman

cut 2

cut 2 feet

* This paper is also available by the sheet

Turtle

- patterned *Paper Pizazz*™: tortoise shell (*Bright Great Backgrounds*)
- solid *Paper Pizazz*™: black (*Solid Jewel Tones*); blue, green (*Plain Brights*); white (*Plain Pastels*)
- black pen: Zig

♥ Mat each piece on black.

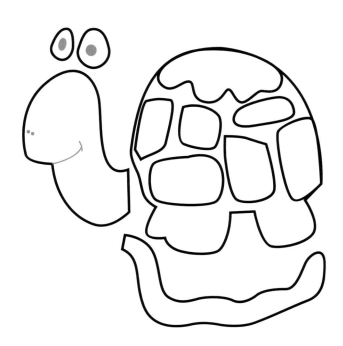

Umbrella

- patterned *Paper Pizazz*™: cherries on white with check border, cherries on black (*Janie Dawson's Sweet Companions*)
- solid *Paper Pizazz*™: black (*Solid Jewel Tones*); red (*Plain Brights*); white (*Plain Pastels*)

♥ Mat each piece as shown.

Uncle Sam

- patterned *Paper Pizazz*™: red pinstripe*, navy checks* (*Dots, Checks, Plaids & Stripes*)
- solid *Paper Pizazz*™: navy blue, black (*Solid Jewel Tones*); white, tan (*Plain Pastels*)
- ¼" star punch: Family Treasures
- red decorating chalk: Craf-T Products
- cotton swab
- black pen: Zig

cut 3 stars

cut 2 cuffs

cut 3 ties

pattern by Ruth Ninneman

* This paper is also available by the sheet

Unicorn

- patterned *Paper Pizazz*™: white moiré* (*Wedding*); yellow roses* (*Romantic Papers*); sepia tiles* (*Making Heritage Scrapbook Pages*)
- solid *Paper Pizazz*™: black (*Solid Jewel Tones*)
- black pen: Zig
- white and blue pens: Pentel

♥ Mat each piece on black.

Wagon

- patterned *Paper Pizazz*™: red with white dots* (*Ho, Ho, Ho!!!*)
- solid *Paper Pizazz*™: black (*Solid Jewel Tones*); red (*Plain Brights*); white (*Plain Pastels*); black (*Solid Jewel Tones*)
- black pen: Zig
- white pen: Pentel

Watermelon Slice

- patterned *Paper Pizazz*™: red with tri-dots*, green check* (*Dots, Checks, Plaids & Stripes*); green velvet (*"Velvet" Backgrounds*)
- solid *Paper Pizazz*™: black (*Solid Jewel Tones*)
- ⅜" long teardrop punch: Family Treasures
- black pen: Zig

cut 7 watermelon seeds

* This paper is also available by the sheet

Witch

- patterned *Paper Pizazz*™: black velvet* (*"Velvet" Backgrounds*); purple swirl, blue swirl, blue and green stripe (*Bright Great Backgrounds*); brown crushed suede* (*Black & White Photos*)
- solid *Paper Pizazz*™: lime green, white, yellow (*Plain Pastels*); orange (*Plain Brights*); black (*Solid Jewel Tones*)
- deckle scissors: Fiskars
- ¼" hole, 1" star punch: McGill, Inc.
- pink decorating chalk: Craf-T Products
- cotton swab
- black pen: Zig
- sliver pen: Pentel

The patterns for the hair, hat, broom, frog and frog's sign are on page 142.

pattern by Nance Wilhite-Kueneman

BROOM RIDES

Witch (cont'd)

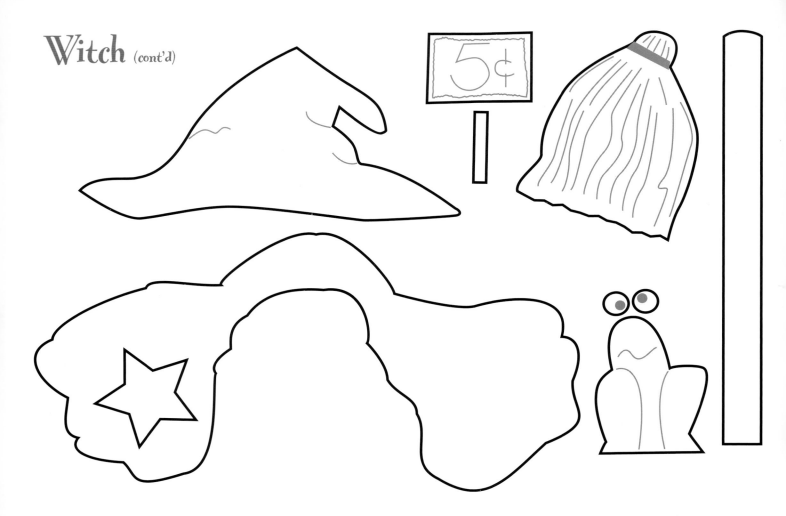

Wizard

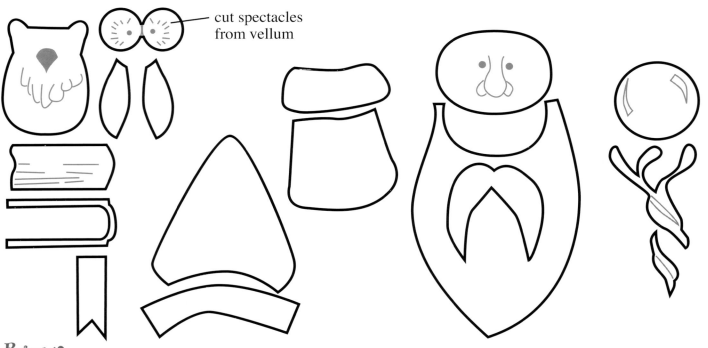

cut spectacles from vellum

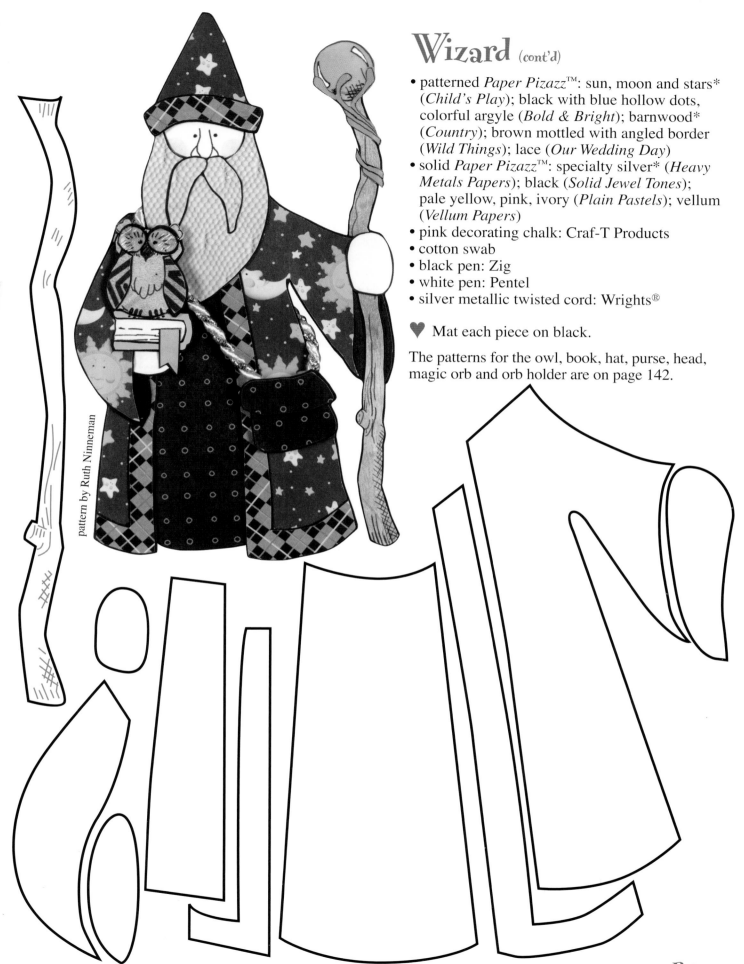

Wizard (cont'd)

- patterned *Paper Pizazz*™: sun, moon and stars* (*Child's Play*); black with blue hollow dots, colorful argyle (*Bold & Bright*); barnwood* (*Country*); brown mottled with angled border (*Wild Things*); lace (*Our Wedding Day*)
- solid *Paper Pizazz*™: specialty silver* (*Heavy Metals Papers*); black (*Solid Jewel Tones*); pale yellow, pink, ivory (*Plain Pastels*); vellum (*Vellum Papers*)
- pink decorating chalk: Craf-T Products
- cotton swab
- black pen: Zig
- white pen: Pentel
- silver metallic twisted cord: Wrights®

♥ Mat each piece on black.

The patterns for the owl, book, hat, purse, head, magic orb and orb holder are on page 142.

pattern by Ruth Ninneman

Manufacturers

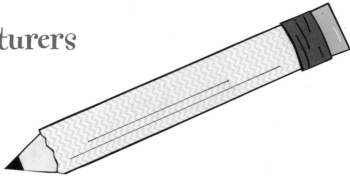

Craf-T Products: decorating chalks
P.O. Box 83
Fairmont, MN 56031
507/235-3996
www.craf-tproducts.com

Dixon Ticonderoga Co.: Prang colored pencils
195 International Parkway
Heathrow, Florida 32746
407/829-9000
www.dixonticonderoga.com

EK Success, Ltd.: Zig gel pens and 2-Way glue
125 Entin Rd.
Clifton, NJ 07014-1141
913/458-0092
www.eksuccess.com

Hot Off The Press: Paper Pizazz™,
Coordinating Colors™, Punch-Outs™
1250 NW 3rd St.
Canby, OR 97013
503/266-9102
www.paperpizazz.com

Family Treasures, Inc.: pattern-edged scissors, punches
Family Treasures, Inc.
24922 Anz Dr., Unit D
Valencia, CA 91355
661/294-1330
www.familytreasures.com

Fiskars, Inc.: pattern-edged scissors
7811 W. Stewart Ave.
Wausau, WI 54401
715/845-3802
www.fiskars.com

Marvy® Uchida: punches
3535 Del Amo Blvd.
Torrance, CA 90503
310/793-2200
www.uchida.com

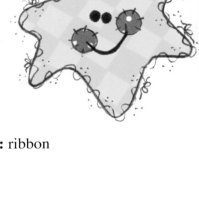

McGill, Inc.: punches
P.O. Box 177
Marengo, IL 60152
815/568-7224
www.mcgillinc.com

C.M. Offray & Son, Inc.: ribbon
Rt. 24 Box 601
Chester, NJ 07930-0601
908/879-4700
www.offray.com

Pentel of America, Ltd.: gel pens
2805 Columbia St.
Torrance, CA 90509
310/320-3831
www.pentel-usa.com

Wrights: cording
85 South Street, PO Box 398
West Warren, MA 01092
413/436-7732
www.wrights.com

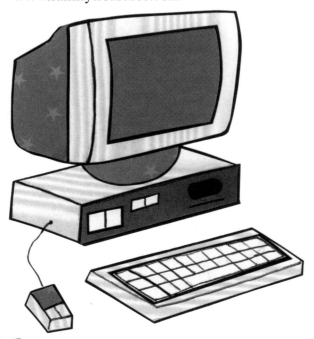